A JOURNAL

OF A

TOUR IN THE CONGO

FREE STATE

A JOURNAL

OF A

TOUR IN THE CONGO

FREE STATE

BY

MARCUS R. P. DORMAN, M. A.

Author of A *History of the British Empire in the Nineteenth Century;*
The Mind of the Nation, a study of political thought
in the Nineteenth Century;
Ignorance, a study of the causes and effects of popular thought
and *From Matter to Mind.*

NEGRO UNIVERSITIES PRESS
WESTPORT, CONNECTICUT

Originally published in 1905
by J. Lebègue and Co., Brussels
and Kegan Paul, Trench, Trübner & Co., Ltd., London

Reprinted in 1970 by
Negro Universities Press
A Division of Greenwood Press, Inc.
Westport, Connecticut

Library of Congress Catalogue Card Number 75-106775

SBN 8371-3531-1

Printed in the United States of America

Dedicated

by

Permission

to

His Majesty Leopold II,

King of Belgium

and

Sovereign of the Congo Free State.

PREFACE.

This journal is practically my Diary reproduced with the minimum of editing in order that the impressions gained on the spot should be described without modification. It was never intended for publication, and was written only as an aid to memory. Consequently it is little more than a collection of rough notes.

Having left England with a prejudice against the Government of the Congo Free State and returned with a very strong feeling in its favour, I feel however that it is my duty to publish an account of what I did see for the benefit of those whose opinions are not already formed beyond recall.

As in all controversies where feelings subordinate reason and people judge more by their emotions than by evidence, many are too quick to-day to attribute interested motives to those whose opinions are not similar to their own. Since a great number of people in the Congo and at home

are curious to know whether I was sent out by the Congo
Government, the British Government or the *Times*, I will
state here once for all that I went to the Congo entirely to
please myself and with the hope of shooting big game. In
order indeed to satisfy curiosity, I will go further and state
that not only was I not paid for telling the truth, but that
the trip cost me a great deal of money.

It is however delightful to remember that wherever I
went I was treated with the greatest kindness and courtesy
by all whether they approved of the system of the Congo
Government or not and it gives me great pleasure to thank
here the State officials, Missionaries of all denominations
and Traders of various nationalities for their hospitality,
friendship and valuable assistance.

M. R. P. D.

London 1905.

THE STEAMER « FLORIDA. »

CHAPTER I.

London to Banana.

There was no time to spare. The ship sailed from Southamptom in forty eight hours and I had only just arranged to accompany Lord Mountmorres on a tour in the Congo Free State. He was going out for the purpose of discovering the true condition of affairs in that country and of writing articles thereupon for the *Globe* but incidentally hoped to have some big game shooting. After one has read much about a country it is always interesting to visit it and as the prospect of good sport was added in this case, I at once decided to brave the cannibals, wild

1

beasts, and—most dangerous of all—the climate, and to seize the opportunity to visit the Congo.

It was necessary to purchase a complete camp outfit, suitable clothes and much food-stuff and to arrange certain affairs at home. The first part was however rendered easy for it was only necessary to duplicate the order already given by Lord Mountmorres, and with a rapidity which could not be equalled anywhere else, the Army and Navy Stores and Messrs. Silvers packed and despatched tent, furniture and cases in a few hours.

As there are many and varied discomforts which cannot be avoided when travelling in the Congo, or any other tropical and half-civilised country, it is just as well not to add to their number by omitting to benefit by the experience of others. A few hints may therefore be inserted here without apology for the benefit of other travellers. The first articles to be considered are a tent, bed, and mosquito-net. Now when the usual oblong tent with a penthouse roof is pitched and the bed made, surmounted by the mosquito-net, the only place in which there is room for it, is in the middle of the tent between the two poles. The result is that as the roof slopes, it is absolutely impossible to stand upright on either side and much space is therefore wasted. It would be better to arrange for the bed to stand close to one side of the tent and for the net to be attached to the sloping roof leaving the middle and the other side free for table and chair. Circles of hooks for clothes should be attached to the poles and large pockets in the walls of the tent itself are useful. It is needless to specify particulars about furniture, and I will only say that the folding or concertina pattern bed,

bath, washhandstand and table proved very comfortable
and withstood the great strain of being packed and unpack-
ed nearly every day for six months without breaking
down. A strong, long lounge chair is absolutely necessary. In climates where there is much glare, everything
should be made of green canvas. The well-known Lord's
patent petrol lamp is certainly the best and although it
necessitates carrying a good supply of oil, is cleaner and
more convenient than candles. There is not space here
to give a list of all the necessities for travelling and camping in the forests of Africa and it is enough to say that one
has to carry a complete house, furniture, kitchen utensils
and much food. Wheat and milk cows do not exist in the
forest and very little grows which is edible. It is therefore
necessary to carry sufficient flour, butter, lard, condi-
ments, tinned meats, vegetables and fruits in order to cook,
and to make a variety from the antelopes, fish, game,
goats and chickens which are procurable on the spot.
Water bottles and filters are very necessary, but for
Africa the best change at home – those which have porcelain cores – are of no use for the water is very muddy,
and the minute pores at once become blocked. The charcoal filters, although bulky to carry, are therefore the best
for the forest. The question of alcohol must be left to the
individual himself, but it must be remembered that there
are only a very few places where it can be purchased in
the Congo and that the State officials are only permitted to
have a limited amount for themselves. Undoubtedly the
best wine for the climate is good claret or burgundy, and
the healthiest spirit, whisky. It is however, well to have
some medical comforts in the shape of champagne and

brandy to take after attacks of fever. Excellent native coffee can be purchased; tea and sugar must be carried. Drugs, especially iron, quinine, arsenic and phenacetin are essential as also splints, bandages and dressings in case of accidents.

Now it must be remembered that the climate is hot and humid. Metals rust at once, leather and cloth become mouldy, food stuffs will keep one or two days only after the tins are opened, and cigars, tobacco and cigarettes become damp and ferment. In packing therefore, all the food, cigars, cigarettes and tobacco should be soldered airtight and in tins so arranged that when once opened, it is possible *to shut* them again. A tin of sardines or condensed milk once opened cannot be carried in a case liable to be upside down at any moment. There are however, some bottles with screw tops and india-rubber rings in which Messrs. Crosse and Blackwell send out jam. These are airtight and so very useful for when they are empty they can be cleaned and used for milk, sardines, or anything else again and again. Messrs. Huntley and Palmer pack biscuits in their usual tins but with an inner lid soldered, and these are also very convenient. Above all things, remember curry powder, pickles, chutney and Worcester sauce, for even goat's flesh can be rendered pleasant if it tastes of something else. All this may sound trivial, but it is really very important, for the appetite is easily lost in the Congo and if the strength is not maintained by plenty of food, sickness is certain to follow. Leather cases for rifles and guns are not good as they deteriorate. The best case I have ever seen was made for me by a ship's boatswain. It was of strong sail canvas made to fit the rifle and covered outside with ordinary ship's paint; the inside speedily became lined with oil and the whole formed an excellent guard against the damp. It is however, necessary to have firearms cleaned and oiled nearly every day whether used or not.

Clothes of cloth are not necessary. Drill, khaki and flannel are sufficient with light helmets and plenty of strong boots. It must be remembered that everything has to be carried by porters. Clothes, blankets, &c. should be packed in tin boxes with rubber edges so that when shut they are airtight; tents pack in bales and every article of furniture should fold up. The whole equipment must be arranged so that each load is about 50 or 60 lbs and is conveniently shaped for carrying on the head or shoulder. We were careful to choose the lightest articles, whenever consistent with strength, and thus our baggage when completed weighed only a little more than two tons.

All was ready when we left Waterloo at 10.25 a. m. on Friday June 24th 1904 accompanied by Sir Alfred Jones and Sir Ralph Moor who saw us off at Southampton. The latter has had much experience of Africa and told some blood-curdling stories of the manners of the natives. Adulterers used to be punished in a most barbarous way. A youth who had erred with one of the numerous wives of a Chief, was nailed by the ears to a tree in the forest and left to starve. Women also were treated with equal severity and all manner of mutilations were practised. Such atrocities have of course been suppressed by the Congo Free State.

Having reached Southampton, we went on board the S. S. *Leopoldville,* a ship of about 5,000 tons burden, very clean and well-found. She belongs to the *Compagnie maritime belge* which runs a ship every third week from Antwerp and Southampton to Boma and Matadi. We sailed about 2 p. m. and a savoury smell from the galley reminded us that it was about seven hours since we had breakfasted.

Some of the passengers were English military officers and miners bound for the Gold Coast, but most were evidently officials of the Congo Free State. The conversation soon turned upon the agitation in Europe against the Congo Government, and it was extraordinary with what sorrowful indignation the various charges were refuted. This impressed me greatly at the time for it was in marked contrast with the indifference shown by an average Englishmen when his country and methods are abused by foreigners. Probably the explanation is, that we are so used to unmerited abuse, that we regard it as part of the normal order of things. The Congo State on the other hand, has only recently become sufficiently prosperous to attract attention.

One of the passengers dressed as a Catholic Priest, proved a veritable mine of information. This was Mgr. Derikx, Prefet Apostolique of Uele in the Upper Congo. He had had five years' experience of the country and was well versed in all its institutions and ways. Another was a young military officer, M. Arnold, already of the rank of Commandant, for he had shown distinguished service in the field—or rather the forest—and also as an administrator at a State Post. There were also many other officials, soldiers, lawyers and commercial agents on board.

I determined therefore, to read the various books and reports written against the Congo—whether the writers had ever been in the country or not — then to question the officials who had worked there, and finally to see the actual condition of affairs for myself.

We tumbled about in the Bay of Biscay a little and the motion did not much aid the digestion of the contents of histories and blue and white books. A welcome break was therefore made when we reached Teneriffe on June 29th. It is early afternoon and the view of Santa Crus from the sea is very beautiful. In the foreground is ultra-marine coloured water; on shore, bright yellow houses with red roofs dotted among palms and other foliage of vivid green, and behind all, frowns the great grey mountain 12,000 feet high. The hills stretching up from the sea are in many cases terraced for gardens and vineyards and a new hotel stands out prominently on one side. It is a glorious picture, but if the eye is delighted as the boat approaches the shore, the nose is offended immediately on landing. Streets, houses and people near the harbour are dirty and odoriferous and as the shops are all shut for a saint's day, the town looks dismal in spite of the bright sun.

After changing some money at the shop of a jew who gave us the wrong amount and looked injured when we insisted upon the right, we took an open carriage and drove to the Cathedral. The building is not imposing from the outside, but is highly gilded within where is the famous Holy Cross which gives the town its name. There are also many wax figures representing saints, mostly dressed in the costume of the seventeenth century and enclosed in glass cases. The boy who acted as our guide having discovered our nationality, pointed out with great

glee « English organ, » « English clock » and finally
with satirical humour—probably unconscious—« English
flags. »   These flags are those lost by Nelson at the seige
of Santa Crus where he lost his arm and a good story is
told about them.   An ambitious British middy stole them
from the Cathedral and was very disappointed, when
instead of being at once promoted, he was forced to apolo-
gize and restore them.

We next drive up a broad, fairly well kept, boulevard
to the Bull Ring situated in an open space behind the
town.   A woman conducts us into the ring and shows us
the stables in which the infuriated beasts are kept before
they are asked to shed their blood for the idle amusement
of the spectators.   On the walls are many names which
look like British, and the guide is quite astonished when
we refuse to add ours to their number.

Commandant Arnold here takes on board six camels,
for it is hoped these ships of the desert will also sail
equally well in the forest.   The experiment is at any rate
not expensive, for they only cost £16 each and will carry
several hundred pounds weight of baggage.

From time to time the Congo Government has been
charged with forcing the natives to work against their will
and with ill-treating them, and it has also been alleged
that the native soldiers committed many atrocities during
the wars against the revolting tribes.   Many of these
charges have been collected and published in *Civilisation
in Congoland* written by Mr. H. R. Fox-Bourne, the
Secretary of the Aborigines Protection Society.   The
author has not travelled in the country himself, but relies
chiefly upon the evidence of the late Mr. Edward Glave,

at one time an official of the Congo International Association, and of the late Mr. Sjöblom who was a Swedish Missionary in the Congo. The book is not cheerful reading, for indeed it is chiefly a record of crimes which have been committed in the past.

It has been frequently stated that acting under the orders, or at least with the connivance of the agents of the Congo State and those of the Commercial Companies in the country, the native police or sentries have punished in a most barbarous manner all those natives who refused to work. It is alleged indeed, that these sentries have actually cut off the hands of those who did not collect the rubber or foodstuff demanded by the agents. To even read of such sickening horrors is terrible, and I was therefore much relieved to find that none of the State officials on board had ever seen natives maimed in that or any other manner by the soldiers of the State. There seems however, to be no doubt that the native chiefs in the past mutilated both the living and dead as punishment for crime. Mgr. Derikx told me that he had heard of a case where a chief had ordered that the hand of his own son should be cut off because he had committed adultery with one of his numerous wives.

We arrived at Dakar, the capital of the French colony of Senegambia, at daylight on July 3rd. Navigation is not easy here, for a reef runs parallel to the coast and the channel between, is neither broad nor deep. The town is built on the shores of a bay and faces an island strongly fortified. The whole colony is being rapidly developed; a railway runs to St. Louis and roads are being constructed across the desert towards Timbuctoo and the northern coasts. A flourishing industry in palm oil is carried on and Dakar is also an important military centre. Several of the officers however, were engaged in the peaceful pursuit of fishing at the end of the breakwater when we arrived.

At Dakar, Commandant and Madame Sillye come on board. The former has served for ten years in the Congo and is now taking out ten horses purchased in Senegambia, from which he hopes to breed. They are a fine looking set, very quiet and well behaved, and take up their quarters opposite the camels without creating any disturbance. We have now quite a menagerie on board. Besides the camels and horses, there are pigeons to be trained as carriers, guinea pigs with which the doctors investigating the terrible disease the Sleeping Sickness, will experiment and several dogs belonging to the passengers. Various kinds of rubber and other living plants also occupy an appreciable part of the promenade deck. Passengers and cargo indeed, are strong evidence of the earnest way in which the Congo is being developed.

It is necessary now to turn from the actual visual facts and to study the statements of others. While doing so however, we must bear in mind the main outlines of the history of the Congo Free State. The opening up of the Congo was entirely due to the initiative of King Leopold of Belgium aided by the explorations of the late Sir H. M. Stanley. In 1878, after Stanley's first descent of the Congo, a society of philanthropists was formed called the *Comité d'études du Haut-Congo* but this was changed in 1882 to the *Association Internationale du Congo*. Stanley and a French officer, M. de Brazza, then both worked up from the coast at the same time and the former reached Lake Leopold on June 1st 1882, while the latter concluded treaties with the Chiefs on the north bank of the river and founded the French Congo.

The International Association of the Congo at once organised itself into an Independent State and on April 22nd 1884 a Declaration was made by the Government of the United States of America that it recognized the flag of the International Association as that of a friendly Government. At the end of 1884 and the beginning of 1885, Conventions were arranged between the Governments of Austria, Germany, Great Britain, Belgium, Denmark, Spain, France, Italy, Holland, Portugal, Russia and Sweden and Norway and the International Association of the Congo in which all those countries recognised the flag of the International Association as that of a friendly Government. It is therefore clear that the chief Powers of the World regarded the Association as an Independent State and negotiated with it as such.

At the same time the Powers of Europe were annexing various parts of Africa, and with the idea of regulating in a spirit of mutual goodwill the conditions most favourable for the development of civilisation and commerce, a Conference was arranged at Berlin by Prince Bismarck. All the Powers of Europe and the United States of America sent plenipotentiaries who sat from November 15th 1884 to February 26th 1885 and agreed to the General Act of Berlin of the latter date. In this it is decreed that all nations should enjoy complete liberty of commerce in all the territories constituting the basin of the Congo and its tributaries, and also in other parts of Central Africa mentioned, that slavery should be abolished and that the Congo river should be open to general navigation.

We shall have to refer to this Treaty later, but it is important to note here that the United States of America and all the great Powers of Europe had recognised the International Association as an Independent State before it was signed. Furthermore, before this date, Conventions had been signed with France and Portugal to arrange the frontiers between the territories of those Powers and the International Association. The General Act of Berlin had however nothing to do with frontiers at all, but stated the general principles which it seemed were best suited to the needs of the people and territories in Central Africa, to which all the African Powers, and among them the International Association, voluntarily agreed. It is therefore clear that the clauses of the Act apply to all the Powers in the territories defined, and that the Act itself was not concerned with founding or regulating the system of Government of the International Association, which six months later took the name of the *État Indépendant du Congo* with His Majesty King Leopold II. as sovereign.

While engaged in studying these treaties, we arrived at Free Town, Sierra Leone on July 5th. Here again the place forms a beautiful picture from the sea. A reef runs far out and is marked by a lighthouse, while the town itself, protected by a fort with grass ramparts, lies on the south side of a kind of bay, which, however, has more the appearance of the mouth of a large river. Palms and other tropical plants grow to the water's edge and among them are yellow and red houses while higher up the hills behind, are isolated bungalows and the barracks, at this time

occupied by the West African regiment. In the distance,
bleak and bare mountains passively regard the scene. On
landing, one meets faces showing every shade from ivory
white to jet black and clothes of every known colour.
The roads are not paved in any way, as there are neither
horses nor wheeled vehicles here. Indeed, the houses are
built in rows facing each other, a gutter is cut in front and
the space between forms a street. The Custom House is
an imposing structure near the beach and the Cathedral is
a handsome Gothic church, but as one end was covered
with scaffolding, it was not looking its best. A light railway runs up the hill to the barracks of the native regiment
and a special train was arranged for the passengers of the
Léopoldville.

Hotel accommodation in Sierra Leone is, like the demand
for it, limited. It is, however, possible to obtain a meal
at the *Victoria.* Altogether Free Town leaves the impression that it could be developed into a most attractive
watering place if it were nearer Europe and had a better
climate.

It is now getting rather hot and tropical, while the sea
is as smooth as a mirror and equally reflects the glare.

I continue to read up the Congo controversy. The
report of Mr. Casement, at one time British Consul at
Boma, created quite a sensation when it appeared. He
stated that the Congo Free State had granted conces-
sions to Trading Companies, which is a fact, and that the
agents of these companies compelled the natives by force
to collect rubber, which however, he does not attempt to
prove by his own experience, but relies entirely upon
reports of natives and hearsay evidence. He quoted one

case which illustrates the extreme difficulty of discovering the truth from natives. He examined a boy named Epondo who stated that his left hand had been cut off by a native sentry. Not knowing the native dialect, Mr. Casement employed an interpreter, but he was convinced by the manner and gestures of the villagers that the boy's story was true. When the report appeared, the boy was again examined by some officials of the State, when he at once contradicted the first statement and said that his arm and hand had been severely bitten by a wild boar when he was a child and that the hand afterwards fell off. Now one of these tales is obviously false and there is evidence to show which, for the scar of a clean cut wound is different from that following gangrene. However, at this time I had not seen the boy, so of course could give no opinion. This is the only case of reputed mutilation which could be discovered for the benefit of Mr. Casement and was a very unfortunate example of an atrocity, for in the first place it was the *left* hand that was missing and the soldiers were supposed always to cut off the *right*, and in the second, there was great doubt whether it was the result of an accident or not.

We were now coasting off Liberia and Captain Sparrow who was in command of the *Leopoldville* cheered us up with the statement that the charts of this part had not been revised for eighty years, that there were many rocks and that ships frequently went ashore here. Wreckers then went out and looted everything on board. It is not therefore, a pleasant place in which to make an enforced landing

Liberia itself however, must be interesting to visit,

for it is an independent republic of negroes with an elected President, Senate and House of Representatives. It sells palm oil to other countries and buys alcohol, arms and ammunition, thus exchanging a peaceful luminant and lubricant for the elements of moral and physical strife. Fortunately no rocks appear through the bottom of the ship and Commandant Sillye relieves the monotony of the voyage by describing the Constitution of the Congo State, which however, like other constitutions, is occasionally revised. At its head is the Sovereign of the State aided by Ministers at Brussels, next in rank comes the Governor-General and Vice-Governor-Generals, one of whom is always at Boma. There are also Royal Commissioners and Inspectors of the State who are very high officials, but whose duties are not easily defined. The whole country is divided into Districts which are governed by District Commissioners. The Districts are divided into zones ruled by zone chiefs under the control of the District Commissioners. Finally the Posts and Stations are commanded by Post-Commanders. All these may be described as civil administrative officials who, subject to the general system and laws have practical control over more or less limited areas. The officers of the Force Publique rank as Commandant, Captain, Lieutenant and Under-Lieutenant, and there are also several white non-commissioned officers. The natives rank as sergeants, corporals and privates.

On July 8th we arrive at Sekondi, Gold Coast Colony. The town from the sea seems to consist of white houses and huts with the usual red roofs. On a hillock near the shore is an old Dutch fort now used as a signalling station, and on the left, half way up a hill, an hotel has been built The place is not very pretty or attractive-looking for there is not much colour and no mountains are visible. We anchor some distance from the beach and several open boats at once put off These are each propelled by ten or twelve natives, who sit on the sides of the boat and ply their paddles, lustily singing as they work together and with a will. The paddles are shaped somewhat like those of a Canadian canoe, except that the blade is star shaped. All the cargo is swung overboard into these boats or canoes as they are called, and the passengers are lowered in a kind of chair. As there is a heavy ground swell running, the canoes are bobbing up and down like corks alongside. The chair is suspended in mid air and lowered rapidly as the canoe washes up, while all hope that it and its occupant will descend at the right moment.

One of the passengers was an English officer, Captain Wheeler, with whom we had played many games of deck cricket on the voyage. First his regulation seventy cubic feet of baggage was lowered — an extraordinary amount, for no one without the aid of a slide rule and logarithms could possibly calculate it—and then he himself made the perilous descent — without a ducking. He would next have 240 miles of train journey to Coomassie and then a walk — or rather a journey in a hammock – for another 300 miles to his station.

We now travel parallel to the Gold Coast which looks hot and uninviting, for there are but few patches of green or trees until Cape Coast Castle is reached. Here is a fort which must have impressed natives and slave dealers greatly in the past, a few houses and an imposing looking church dotted in the red sand. The whole line of the Coast here, somewhat recalls the Atlantic sea board of Georgia, U. S. A. and the towns look as though they would be as hot as Aden at its best or rather worst.

After leaving the Gold Coast, our course is shaped across the Bight of Benin straight for the Congo. There is plenty of time therefore, to study the system of justice in the Congo. This, like everything else in the country, is essentially simple and practical. There is a Court of Première Instance at Boma and others called Territorial Courts at Matadi, Stanley Pool, East Kwango, The Equator, Bangalas, Aruwimi, Stanley Falls and Kassai (1). In each Court is a Judge, an Officer of the Public Ministry and a Registrar, but in the Territorial Courts, the judge may assume the functions of all. These courts hear all civil cases, whether European or native, but the Court at Boma is alone competent to hear trials for capital offences, whether committed by soldiers or civilians. The Court of Appeal consists of the President, two Judges, an Officer of the Public Ministry and a Registrar, and hears all appeals from the judgments of the other Courts, and also from those given by Courts Martial against civilians who are not natives in those regions subjected to special rule. Natives who commit offences against other natives, are left to be dealt with by the local Chief (2). The Public Minister can

---

(1) This list is taken from *Justice Repressive* (*État Indépendant du Congo*) and is based on a Decree of 1896. Since then other Territorial Courts have been or are about to be added.

(2) Some of the greater Chiefs and Sultans have the power to inflict the death sentence.

however interfere if he thinks the crime will not be punished if left to the Chief.

The Public Ministry consists of a Procureur d'État appointed by the Sovereign, who acts in the Court of Appeal and of substitutes appointed by the Governor General, who act in the other Courts. Their duty is to discover all infractions of the law in the whole territory of the State and to see that all decrees, arrests, ordinances and penal regulations are carried out. They are especially instructed to arrange that any native who has been injured receives full compensation before any fine is taken to the profit of the State.

Any region can be placed under military law by a decree of the Governor General. Civilians however, are only subject to the ordinary penal laws, and those who are not natives, can appeal against any decision of a Court Martial. In practice these simple methods work admirably and it is difficult to understand why they should not be equally successful in old civilised countries and a good substitute for the complicated and cumbrous machinery of to-day.

THE NATIVE HOSPITAL AT BOMA.

CHAPTER II.

Banana to Leopoldville.

The amount of sand in the bath water on the morning
of July 12th indicated that we were approaching the
mouth of a large river. The Atlantic indeed, which had
varied in colour from dirty green near the English Channel
to ultra marine at Teneriffe, was now of a fine amber tint.
As yet land was not in sight; it was comparatively cool
and a slight breeze was blowing. About midday the low
lying coast of Central Africa became visible as a dark line
and half an hour afterwards a simple break could be seen
in this line which was the clearly defined mouth of the

Congo. On reference to the chart it became clear that although the lower Congo forms a delta in some places twenty miles in width, all the streams coalesce and flow through an opening not more than five miles wide. On both sides the coast is low lying and well wooded.

As we approach nearer, the northern point resolves itself into the extremity of a peninsula, for one branch of the river turns northward thus leaving a strip of land a few hundred yards wide. We pass through the mouth of the river, thread our way between several buoys, turn up this northern channel and arrive at an anchorage in which eight or nine small ships are riding. As we take up our position a boat leaves the shore flying the Congo Flag, a blue ground with a golden star in the centre. Soon after we go ashore in a « dug out » propelled by Kru boys to the town of Banana, which is built on this sandy peninsula and is thus guarded by sharks on one side and crocodiles on the other. We land at a wooden pier used chiefly for loading canoes. On each side are magnificient palms, some being more than fifty feet high and all bearing many cocoa nuts at this season about half ripe. These palms are not indigenous, but flourish here. The main highway of Banana is a path of clean yellow sand about ten feet wide, shaded by an avenue of these palms and crosses at intervals small tidal streams by rustic wooden bridges. Many tropical trees and shrubs grow on each side of the avenue, and in the bright sunshine the whole forms a very beautiful picture. It is unfortunate that the effect reminds one somewhat forcibly of a transformation scene of a pantomime and thus appears artificial although in reality, it is absolutely natural. The resemblance is still further strengthened by the numerous ladies of the ballet who leisurely stroll along clothed in nature's ebony black. No one seems to know the origin of the name of the town, for the Banana palm is not found here at all.

At the extreme end of the point, and extending inwards for several hundred yards, are the grounds of the Dutch Trading Company, which has been established here for more than fifty years and ships many of the products of the country. The wooden sheds painted white are very picturesque amid the vivid green foliage. Beyond this area is the house of Dr. Carré, the Commissaire of the District of Banana, which like all the other houses in the town is raised on piles above the level of the sand, for the double purpose of ensuring a current of air beneath and of keeping it dry when the peninsula is flooded. It faces the sea and behind is a small garden in which are many meteorological instruments. Among these are an anemometer slowly revolving in the light air, maximum and minimum bulbs in the shade, on the ground and beneath it, a most ingenious sun dial, and a heliometer. Walking inland along the central avenue, we pass some native shops, one of which bears the interesting name of *Williams Brothers*. In many of the verandahs, native women wrapped in highly coloured cloths but with bare feet and legs, are working sewing machines or tending their children. Further on is a space laid out in regular squares, in each of which is a well built wooden house raised on piles, and an ornamental garden, the flower beds being bordered either with sea shells or with glass bottles pushed neck downwards into the sand, leaving about two inches projecting above the surface. A little further on is

an hotel facing the sea in which is apparently poor accommodation and not much to eat or drink.   Beyond this is
the native village, consisting of square huts and rough
gardens in which some potatoes seem to be growing in
spite of the soil and temperature.

Only about twenty Europeans live at Banana and their
chief excitement is the arrival of the steamer.   Most of
them indeed came off to dinner and held a kind of concert
in the saloon afterwards.   All night long winches and
men were creaking, groaning, and shouting, as some of
the cargo was put overboard into two large lighters.   It
was not however, destined for Banana and was trans-
shipped here only to lighten the *Léopoldville* so that she
could pass a certain bar higher up the river.   The cargo
consisted of coal in the shape of brickets, cement, rice,
oil, cloth, clothes, beads, salt and general provisions.
As soon as sufficient had been removed, the two lighters
were attached one to each side of the ship and we started
up the main stream, which here runs between the south or
Portuguese bank and a series of islands.   All these are
covered with dense forest the only living things visible
being great black eagles with white wings.   On the left
bank of the river we pass Malela, a station for collecting
bamboos, and soon after Kissange on the opposite side
where palm oil is made and shipped.   A little higher up,
the country opens out and a range of hills becomes visible
in the distance, the plain between being covered with
coarse grass six or seven feet high, relieved at intervals
by solitary palm trees.   This is all Portuguese territory,
the Congo State here possessing only a narrow strip of
land along the northern bank.   The course of the river

here is very sinuous, winding in and out among the hills,
the curves being cut more sharply each day as the water
eats into the sand and carries it to be digested in the great
stomach of the Atlantic

In this district both the State and the Portuguese have
started large farms for breeding European cattle which
thrive here satisfactorily.   Higher up a solitary rock
overhangs the left bank.   This is known as Fetish Rock
from the legend that the natives used to throw live people
from it into the river as sacrifices.   This is possibly true
but there is little evidence to show that the natives of the
Congo ever sacrificed either living or dead to propitiate
anyone or anything.

Near here we anchor for the night and are welcomed by
a host of most noisy and vicious mosquitoes who have a
particular partiality to good healthy European-fed blood.
Again we are delayed to unload and this time into a small
steamer the *Lagoon* – for the ship is still too deep in the
water to cross the bar.   This sandy obstruction has an
unpleasant habit of shifting its position and it is necessary
therefore to make careful soundings every voyage at this
time of the year when the water is low.   These are carried
out by Captain Sparrow and Mr. Wright the chief Congo
pilot with the aid of a most ingenious sounding machine.
It consists of a simple pulley wheel raised on a standard
about ten feet above the deck of a small pilot steamer.
Over this passes a line weighted at both ends but unequally,
and both weights hang down in the water, the heavier
naturally being on the bottom of the river.   To prevent
this line—which corresponds to the ordinary lead line—
trailing, as the boat moves forward, a second line is

fixed to the weight and passes under water to the bows
of the vessel where it is attached. As the vessel passes
slowly through the water, the weight rises and falls
according to the level of the bottom, and the counterweight
hauls in the slack of the line, which is marked in the
usual way by coloured tapes. At any moment therefore,
the depth of water can be determined by observing the
tapes. There is now only $15\frac{1}{2}$ feet on the bar, so it is
necessary to lighten the *Leopoldville* still more before
it will be possible to cross. Thus early one of the chief
difficulties in the Congo the transport of goods—is
demonstrated.

A fine crocodile lies asleep on the bank within easy
range as we go back to the ship in the launch, but no
one has a rifle so his dreams are undisturbed. As the
Leopoldville wil not be able to reach Boma until the morrow,
we decide to go on in the « *Heron*, » a small ship which
calls for all the « State » passengers. After Fetish Rock,
the river bends sharply to the right and soon after Boma
is in sight. At this distance however, the town merely
appears as groups of white houses amid trees backed by
green hills. Guarding the approach is a strong looking
fort which already has a history, for it was captured by
rebels and held for one or two days a few years ago.

As the sun was seeking his couch we arrive at the
iron pier at Boma on which we find Mr. Underwood, the
Director of the well known English trading house of
Messrs. Hatton and Cookson. With him we walk down
the main business street of the town; a wide shady road
lined with shops, hotels, and restaurants and traversed by
a steam tram. At the end of this street the road continues

to the right, up an incline and opposite to the corner is one of the entrances to the Residency. Passing this we leave a Catholic church, constructed of corrugated iron, on the right and enter a shady avenue in which is the Secretariat. We are then introduced to Mr. Vandamme, the Secretaire General, who at once takes us to the Residency and presents us to Mr. Costermans, the Governor General of the Congo Free State, who hopes we shall travel wherever we feel inclined and see anything we desire.

The Residency is a large two storey house surrounded by a wide verandah and is built of iron plates bolted together. It is raised about ten feet from the ground on iron pillars and approached by a wide staircase with wooden steps. It is surrounded by a well kept garden in which are some statues and many tropical plants. The view from the verandah, looking up and down the river is very pretty. Although the house is in good condition and the dining room large enough to seat thirty people, it is thought not to be worthy of its function, and another large building will soon be erected on the same site.

After this visit we proceed to a house which is kept for the use of the higher State Officials when they pass through Boma and which was now placed at our disposal. It is constructed in a similar manner to the Residency and although smaller, contains three lofty reception and two bed rooms. Two « boys » are told off to attend to our wants and after a rest we take a stroll round the town with Mr. Vandamme. Most of the official residencies are situated in one Avenue and are surrounded by gardens in which palms, bulbous trees, and acacias give welcome shade to the roses beneath. The Avenue du Plateau leads up a gentle incline to the Law Courts in which once a week sits the Court of Première Instance. Near by is the prison and the terminus of the tramway. From the summit of the hill a grand view is obtained of the river winding between the hills to the East, and at one's feet is a native village nestling in a valley, for the natives dislike wind and cold almost as much as they do rain. Separated from it is another native village in which the Government has placed the educated people who can read and write and many are now ambitions to qualify for admission.

It is now time to return to dinner with Mr. Vandamme where we meet Mr. Gohr, the Director of Justice, and Mr. Underwood. Everyone here dines in white, which is both cool and picturesque. Our host has an excellent native cook who gives us some very good vegetable soup, one of the numerous Congo fishes, all of which are nice, a very tender chicken, an excellent salad and a well made omelette, all of which are products of the country. Flour and butter have however, to be imported, as no wheat will grow in this part of the country and the cows give scarcely enough milk for their calves. Everyone retires and rises early, so at 9 p. m. we seek our house guided by a boy with a lantern, for most of the streets of Boma are not lighted artificially.

Next day we call on Mr. Nightingale who is at present acting as British Consul. The consulate is about a mile from the town situated on the banks of the river and is well constructed of wood. Mr. Nightingale offers kindly to lend us any assistance on our voyage that we may require. Afterwards we buy many things which will be necessary up country, among which are bags of salt, a very popular form of money in some parts, and tins of petrol for the lanterns.

Everyone in Boma works hard, from the Secretaire General who is at his office from 7 a. m. to midday and from 2.30 to 5 p. m. to the hardy healthy-looking native who wields his pick as he chats with his fellows. Roads are being made and gardens laid out in various places. One very noticeable feature of the natives here, is that they nearly all bear wellmarked vaccination marks. Here and there a policeman patrols in an effective costume of blue and red and armed with a short sword. Everywhere is order, method, and cleanliness, and it is very difficult to realise that a quarter of a century ago only three trading houses stood on the site of this prosperous and well-regulated little town. In the evening we dined with the Governor General who has both a good cook and butler; the wines being excellent. Outside, the band of the Force Publique played selections of music, rendered the more interesting by the fact that not one of the players could read a note of music and each learnt his part entirely by ear. Most of the guests were our fellow travellers and well known to us. The conversation turned upon the Sleeping Sickness, Beri Beri, the difficulty of growing wheat in the Congo, and the climate. It is not very hot in Boma about this time, for it is the winter or dry season and the nights are so cold that only the very hardy mosquitoes are sufficiently wide awake to prevent people sleeping. Still it is hotter, than we ever experience in England, and with forethought for the comfort of his guests, Mr. Costermans usually commands white costumes instead of European dress.

The native hospital is a newly-built stone and brick structure and is under the charge of an Italian, Dr. Zerbini. The wards are well arranged in separate wings, permitting good ventilation and isolation. The beds are iron with bamboos stretched lengthwise, thus forming a kind of spring mattress. There are many cases of Sleeping Sickness in the hospital exhibiting various symptoms. In the early stages the patient has many fits of emotional excitement and these alternate with periods of physical and mental languor. Afterwards he lies for weeks or months as if dead and can only be persuaded to eat with great difficulty. Ultimately complete coma supervenes. A motile bacillus has been discovered which is supposed to cause the disease and there is evidence that this may be carried by a mosquito or fly, but until the discoveries of the doctors, sent out by the Liverpool School of Tropical Medicine, are published, it is premature to give an opinion. Up to the present many remedies have been prescribed without success. There is no small pox and little phthisis, and it is interesting to learn that appendicitis is unknown in Africa. Rupture is very common among the natives and venereal diseases are frequent.

As I was destined to become well acquainted with the *Croix rouge*, the hospital for Europeans, I will describe this institution later. On the reverse slope of the central hill of Boma are the quarters of the army, the Force Publique. The soldiers are fine looking fellows with a very pretty uniform; blue wide cut breeches to the knee, the legs and feet being bare, blue shirt with red facings and belt, and a red fez. They are armed with Albini rifles, a very strong weapon which will stand any amount

of rough usage. Everything is scrupulously clean and the
married quarters especially look very comfortable. Each
couple has a room fitted with bed, table and chairs.
They are recruited from all over the country and the service is so popular that in many parts far more men
volunteer to serve than are required. The force does not
exceed 13,600 in number and is recruited for long or
short service.

The prison is situated on the plateau in an open, airy
place. The building is constructed of iron plates and the
separate cells and rooms are lofty and clean. There are
one or two Europeans here who have been sentenced for
theft or for cruelty to natives, for the State is determined
that all its subjects should be well treated. These are of
course kept entirely separate from the natives. Only the
natives who have been sentenced to more than one year are
sent here and then after a time they are forwarded to the
penal settlements. Some are cannibals, but most are
thieves, and all wear light chains. It is somewhat warm
walking about Boma but there is no alternative, for there
are no carriages and only a horse or two for the Governor
General. The State regulates very strictly the importation
of arms. Permission has to be obtained from the Governor
General before any fire arms can be landed; then each
one is stamped on the butt with the Star of the State
and a number which is registered. If anyone in the
country wishes to purchase a weapon from another, both
buyer and seller have to obtain permission from the
Governor General. These laws are very excellent for they
effectually keep modern weapons out of the hands of the
natives. Having complied with the regulations and declared

our ammunition, our rifles and guns are restored to us
with pretty little souvenir marks on the butts. We next
apply for a special licence to shoot big game, and this is
promised, but as it takes time to prepare will be sent up
country after us.

The import duty on alcohol is very heavy and runs up to
47 per cent. *ad valorem* and no still of any kind is
permitted to be set up in the country. Beyond Matadi
indeed, special permission has to be obtained before
Europeans can carry any spirituous liquors, and then they
have to declare that it is not for sale to the natives. Heads
of commercial houses are made responsible for the obser-
vance of this law by their employés and the State officials
themselves are only permitted to have three litres of spirits
each month, while absinthe is entirely prohibited. Every
white man, however, is given one litre of red wine each
day as a ration and there seems to be no limit to the
amount of beer which may be drunk, except its great price,
for a bottle of lager costs 3 francs at Leopoldville and
twice that amount higher up the river.

It is indeed becoming apparent that the Government is
a veritable parent and a stern one also. However, as we
promise to be good boys we are permitted to carry a few
cases of whisky and wine — after paying the duty - to
act as « medical comforts » in case of sickness. These
medical comforts are also a feature of the State, each white
being allowed a bottle or two of champagne and port
every three months. Every official indeed receives much
kindness and consideration from the State but is severely
punished any lapse of duty. The whites are fined for care-
lessness or negligence, by stopping their pay for a certain

number of days, and for serious offences any official may be revocated, when he will perhaps lose six months' or even a years' pay. Offences against the penal laws are of course punished by imprisonment.

An excellent institution in Boma is the *colonie scolaire* where foundlings are reared and educated. Orphans, deserted children, half-castes, all are received and trained for some useful purpose, some entering the army, some engaging on the plantations, some becoming servants to the officials.

It is impossible to form any idea of the Congo native in Boma, for the blacks are of very different nationalities. Natives from Lagos, Sierra-Leone, Portuguese and French territory, all are attracted by the high wages to be earned in the town. Indeed at present most of the positions of responsibility, requiring a fair education, are held by foreign blacks, for very few true Congolese can be trusted. The personal servants we engaged were thus all foreigners in the State service. Two rejoiced in the names of Chikaia and Jean, and acted as « boys » *i. e.* as valets, butlers and general servants while Luembo was cook, and Mavunga, washerman. Each one had a formal contract of five articles signed by us, by a delegate for the Governor General, and by the Judge of Première Instance, whose duty it was to see the contract was not broken. The State indeed, superintends everything even to the finding and engaging of private servants for travellers. The wages earned by these boys are very much higher than servants receive in India or China. The cook was paid 35 francs and the others 25 francs per month and all found.

The Customs, the Post Office, and the Land Office, are all conveniently situated in one building on the beach near to the landing pier. In the latter, all the landowners in the State are registered, careful maps being prepared showing the extent and position of each plot of land. The land laws are very simple. The villages are the absolute freehold property of the natives, and are registered in the names of the Chiefs. Vacant lands as usual are the property of the State and the Chartered Companies, Missionaries, and Traders, as a rule, are annual leaseholders but the lease is always renewed if the conditions on which it is granted are observed.

On Sunday we lunched with the Governor General, Mr. Gohr, the Director of Justice—who at present is in the unenviable position of having many critics in Europe, usually imperfectly informed of the details and evidence laid before the judges—Mr. Vandamme, who knows everyone and everything connected with the State, Commandant and Madame Sillye, Judge and Madame Webber, and some others. Afterwards, Mr. Webber, the Judge of the Court of Première Instance, who is an excellent pianist, gives us proof of his talent. This is the last pleasant music we are fated to hear for many a month, for nothing but concertinas and gramophones are found in the interior.

Having obtained bundles of permits to do various things, and arranged for letters and parcels to be sent after us into the interior, we left Boma on the morning of July 19th for Matadi in the « Leopoldville ». The Congo just above Boma somewhat resembles the Highlands of Scotland, and the similarity was emphasised by the fact that

THE CATARACTS RAILWAY NEAR MATADI.

it was raining hard.   The hills were bare of trees, the
current ran rapidly, forming whirlpools, while many sleepy
crocodiles lazily flopped into the water as we passed.   After
ascending some twenty miles, the river turns sharply to the
right and runs between cliffs which descend sheer into the
water, forming a narrow chasm not more than half a mile
broad.   As the whole of the immense volume of water in
the Congo has to pass through this gorge, it is enorm-
ously deep and the current is very rapid.   The depth has
not been accurately ascertained, but it is certainly 500 feet,
if not more, and the flow of the water is at the rate of nearly
ten knots an hour, so that the smaller steamers cannot
ascend at all, and the larger only creep slowly up.

THE RAILWAY STATION AT MATADI.

Matadi is soon after in sight.   It is built on the south
side of the Congo valley, for, as a glance at the map will

3

explain, the State owns both banks at this point, but
further up, the river becomes the frontier with the French
Congo.   Matadi is an ancient — if the word may be used
in connection with the Congo at all — settlement, constructed at the point where navigation on the river is interrupted
by cataracts and rapids for some two hundred miles until
smooth water is reached again at Stanley Pool.   A caravan
route runs from Matadi to Leopoldville, and it was during
the march of twenty days over the mountains that in the
early days, so much trouble was occasioned by the native
porters.   All this is abolished now by the railway.   The
town itself stands on the side of a steep hill and consists of
narrow streets paved with cobbles.   Here as usual in the
Congo, man is restricted to his primeval method of locomo-
tion.   Two iron piers jut into the stream and at their ends
the European steamers discharge their cargoes into the
railway trucks alongside.   High up on the hill stands a
capacious stone structure, the house of the Commissioner of
the Matadi District, Mr. De Rache, with whom we dine.
after arranging to leave by the train which starts next day.
The distance to be traversed is 220 miles and the fare is
£8 each 1st. class and £1 second for the boys.   Besides
this, baggage over a hundred kilos, is charged at the rate
of one franc a kilo, which is probably the highest rate paid
for railway travelling in the world.   Our fares indeed cost
us about £80.

   Early in the morning of the 20th, we leave Matadi.
The train consists of two engines, two open covered carriages for the second class passengers, who are mostly
natives, a saloon and baggage wagon.   The gauge is a
very narrow one, so space is all-important, but the man

who designed the chairs in the saloon must have exercised
the most fiendish ingenuity to make them as uncomfortable
as possible.   There are six on each side, arranged in
pairs with a small bracket table in between, and each one
is on a pivot.   The back is straight upright and the seat
is of cane, cone-shaped, the highest point being in the
centre.   Now as the curves and gradients of the line are
very sharp indeed, it is necessary to hold fast the whole
time, to prevent slipping on to the floor.   If one puts
a foot on the opposite seat to steady oneself, it at once
revolves, leaving the leg in mid air.   However, we fix ourselves in as well as possible and enjoy the magnificent
scenery.   For a few hundred yards the line runs along the
valley of the Congo and a good view of the lowest cataract
is obtained, the brown water dashing over the rocks and
throwing up spray which is converted into brilliant jewels by
the youthful sun not yet an hour old.   Then turning sharply to the right, the train runs up the valley of the Posu, a
mountain torrent which rushes and roars through a narrow
defile.   Snorting angrily, the engines climb up this steep
gradient, cross the river by an iron bridge and then groaning
under the brakes, slide down into another valley.   The main
direction however, is upwards, and as the country opens
out below, one gets a first impression of the enormity and
grandeur of Central Africa.   As far as the eye reaches,
are ranges of hills, the Palabala Mountains crowned by a
great cone which appears first on one side then the other,
as we cork-screw our way up.   The line indeed is a
marvel of engineering construction, for a most difficult
piece of country is traversed without a single tunnel and
with very few cuttings and embankments.   The length of

the railway is, of course, very much greater than a straight line would be between the same points, for it frequently countermarches backwards and forwards up a hill side, and after a detour of perhaps a quarter of a mile, comes back to the same place, but thirty or forty feet higher up. The company which undertook the task of building the line met with many difficulties, but finished it at a cost of £3,000,000 and many native lives. It was built between the years 1891 and 1897 and the workmen were recruited from Senegal and the British Colonies of Africa. Frequent stops are necessary for the engines to drink and gain their second winds, for their work here is very arduous. After two or three hours, however, a plateau is reached and the line runs for miles through dense forests of palms, acacias and « parasol » trees (native Motumbi). The name exactly describes these trees, for the branches are arranged like the ribs, and the leaves spread out and form the covering of the sunshade.

Between the belts of forests the country is covered with coarse grass, six or seven feet high, dotted here and there with palms. No vestige of animal life is visible and only a few natives who are engaged on the railway. These inhabit villages near at hand, formed of huts built of reeds or bamboo and thatched with grass. The men wear a loin cloth only, but the women are wrapped in a plain piece of richly coloured cloth which reaches from the neck to the ankle leaving the arms and feet bare. This is evidently a simple length of stuff some three or four feet wide and, to the masculine eye at least, its method of support remains a mystery, for no trace of button, hook or pin is apparent. Their faces are of the negroid type with broad noses and thick lips and the figures of the women approach the shape of an S reversed thus Ƨ and are similar to those which our American cousins have so largely developed. The men are as a rule thin and tall with very long legs and all appear to have only small arches to their feet. On the lower Congo however, there are many foreigners and several other types are visible. As far as one can judge by the railway cuttings, the soil on the plateau is coarse sand and gravel containing iron and quite unsuitable for agricultual purposes under such a hot sun. The air however, as we approach Tumba, about 2000 feet above sea level, is dry and fresh and at 4 p. m. we halt there for the night.

We are met by Commandant Delhaz, the Commissaire of the Cataracts District, who kindly places a bungalow at our disposal for the night and shows us round the settlement. There is only a small native village here, but large barracks consisting of lines of clean, clay huts constructed by the soldiers. Tumba is indeed an important military centre and here again the appearance of the troops is very fine as they march to the strains of the band which renders snatches from *Faust, Carmen* and other well known airs with a few native variations. A farm has been established in the neighbourhood to feed the garrison and an automobile road is in course of construction.

Next morning, we dress by candle light and make a hasty breakfast, in the midst of which, at 6 a. m., reveille sounds and the troops assemble in the square in front of the Residency. Half an hour afterwards, the train starts, and having perched ourselves on the summits of the seats, we soon reach Sonna Gongo the half-way house for travellers of the future. Here is a depot for locomotives and carriages and wooden hotels are being constructed to accommodate travellers who, after August, will stop here for the night instead of at Tumba.

Leaving Sonna Gongo, the line rapidly searches for a lower level and the view is magnificent, as a great endless expanse of land is unfolded. Here and there are banks of smoke caused by the veldt fires and often close to the railway the high dry grass has been lighted by-a chance spark from an engine, and is burning furiously. We now zigzag down hill instead of up and far beneath, can be seen the thin line of rails glistening in the sun like fillets of silk. Having reached this level, we plunge through inviting looking forests at one time full of elephants, buffaloes and other game, but practically deserted now save by monkeys and parrots.

Soon after the train stops at a station where the natives have assembled to sell fruit and kwanga, a kind of bread made from the flour of the manioc root and the chief article of native diet. It consists chiefly of starch and is not unpleasant when fresh and toasted. The natives however, prefer all food in a high stage of decomposition and it is some time before the very smell of it ceases to make one feel ill. To see them eating kwanga fish or the flesh of elephants, monkeys, antelopes or other animals generally both rotten and raw is most disgusting and brings home the fact sharply that man here is of a very low type.

The oranges the natives sell are very acid, more resembling grape-fruit than the orange of Florida, but the bananas are as good as any in the world and the pine

apples — three of which can be bought for half a franc — are
equal to the finest hot-house variety.

The line now descends again until it reaches a flat hot,
sandy and uninteresting plain across which it runs absolutely straight for seven miles until it reaches Kinshasa on
the South bank of Stanley Pool   A few miles further on,
is the rail head, Leopoldville.   Like everything else in the
Congo, this town has been arranged and built for practical

THE STEAMER « FLANDRE. »

use.   The railway runs along the beach so as to facilitate
the loading and unloading of the steamers of the upper
river, and in a very short time all our baggage is taken
from the train and carried straight on board the *Flandre*
where we find cabins booked for us.   This is an excellent
arrangement and saves much trouble, for although the
steamer does not sail for two days, passengers are allowed

to live on board while in port. Indeed it is very necessary, for there are no hotels in the town, and no accommodation for visitors except a few rooms in the commercial
houses.

Some traits of the native's character were now to be
demonstrated to us. His main idea always is, to do as little
work as possible and he will often take the greatest trouble
in his effort to accomplish this object. Each native endeavoured to put his load as near the gangway as possible which
was soon blocked and then he had to come back, hoist the
package on his head again and carry it to its proper place.
Although this performance took place every day, unless an
officer was constantly on the watch, the foolish fellows
in their attempts to shirk duty brought upon themselves
extra work. The cabins were unfurnished, for everyone
carries his own bed on the Congo, and most also their
own tent. It was therefore necessary to unpack a bed.
Here was a difficulty. All the bags and boxes were
carefully numbered by the Army and Navy Stores andt
he invoice no doubt sent to my London address but I
left before it arrived, and there was no possibility of
discovering which number meant bed. Seizing a likely
looking bale, the boys unlace it, and find a part of a tent, and
a second attempt brings to light another part of a tent. It is
now growing dark and a light is necessary, but in which
of these seventy odd cases is the lamp? Not knowing the
native mind, I explain that it is necessary to hurry and find
the bed before dark. This evidently conveys no meaning
at all to the boys, for in the first place it was not their bed
and so it mattered nothing to them, and in the second, they
had never hurried before in their lives, and could not do so

now, even if they wished. Lacing the first bales up slowly
and deliberately, they open another and find a canvas bath
and washhandstand. These are at any rate useful, and
encouraged by success we try again and come across hand-
irons and starch. At length we find a thing like a large
concertina which is really a folding bed with pillows
and blankets, complete. By great good luck a mosquito
curtain is then found and the steward kindly lends a
candle.

Hot, sticky, tired and cross we prepare for our first
meal on a Congo steamer. It consisted of a soup of
mystery, chicken, which had been washed in the river
close to a group of natives bathing and a goat, killed an
hour before dinner, whose flesh was thrown quivering into
the pot. However, there was some bread and tinned
peaches and it was no use being fastidious in Central
Africa. This was washed down with the regulation half
litre of red wine, a kind of claret which is quite drinkable
and some native coffee which had a delicate and fine
aroma, but was badly made.

The captain—as indeed are nearly all the officers of the
river steamers—was a Scandinavian and spoke English
very well. He explained that the ship was not very clean
or inviting-looking, which was the truth, but as the
lower deck was lumbered up with the horses of Commandant Sillye and was swarming with natives, it was only to
be expected.

Then to bed, but not to sleep, for the boys to save themselves trouble, had not fixed the mosquito net properly.
In my innocence I merely ordered them to do it and had
not stood by and watched. It is indeed necessary always

to see that the native does as he is told, for the moment one's back is turned, he is eating if there is anything rotten enough at hand to tempt him and if not, he quietly goes to sleep. Even these State servants who speak the native language and also a kind of French, really live the lives of animals, for they eat, drink, and sleep if left alone and only work when they are shown how, and watched all the time.

The result was that I spent a most horrible night, for the mosquitoes were terribly hostile and evidently recognised a new European with some healthy blood. In the morning, my head, which I had had shaved in the Congo fashion, was covered with large bumps and face, neck, hands and wrists were all blotches. It was therefore with little appetite that I sat down to a breakfast of bread, dutch cheese, curious tinned butter and weak coffee without milk. Little however, did I think then that in six short months a Congo steamer would seem like a first class hotel, so entirely is everything altered by comparison.

CATARACTS AT LEOPOLDVILLE.

CHAPTER III.

The Higher Congo.

Next day we make a formal call on M₁. Mahieu, Inspecteur d'Etat of the Congo State, whose headquarters are at Leopoldville. He is a very busy man with a multitude of duties, for the paternal system is continued all through the State and the most trivial matters are always referred to the highest official in the neighbourhood. As we are to lunch at the Residency, we do not stay long, but take a ride with Commandant and Mᵐᵉ Sillye on four of the horses the former purchased at Dakar. Although a little stiff after their holiday of a month, they have not been otherwise

affected by their sea voyage and two days in the train.
Along the beach are many steamers charging and discharging and others on the slips being repaired or partly built.
These steamers are all brought out in sections and put
together on the beach. They are flat bottomed, are
driven by stern wheels and only draw three or four feet
of water. They all burn wood, and special depots are
formed at intervals on the rivers where stores of this fuel
are collected. Should however, a steamer run short, it is
only necessary to stop and send the crew ashore with
knives for the banks are lined with forest.

Leaving the beach we ride through avenues of palms
and mango trees to higher ground, whence a beautiful
view can be obtained of Stanley Pool. This is really a
part of the river about sixteen miles wide, shut in by hills
on each side, but its size is not apparent from the water
itself, as a great number of islands cut the stream into
numerous narrow channels. Towards the south, the river
narrows again and at this point is the uppermost of the
cataracts, the water hurling itself against the rocks in its
efforts to escape and recoiling in spray high into the air.
From just below Leopoldville all the way to Matadi, the
river indeed rushes down narrow gorges, but above, for
nearly a thousand miles, it is navigable for steamers. On
a hill above the rapid, is a large tree under which Stanley
pitched his tent and which still bears his name.

Many native villages exist near Leopoldville, consisting
of huts formed of wooden frames and thatched with grass.
There are no plantations or factories here but great numbers of natives are at present employed in road making
and in constructing a new slip for launching the steamers.

Evidently our little party gives rise to much comment for several of the natives have probably never seen a horse before, and a cavalcade of four of these strange animals is something entirely new. On our way back to the ship we pass down the main street in which are the administrative offices, the mess, the doctors' and other private houses and close to the beach, the Residency, over which flies the State flag and in front of which patrols a sentry. At first one thought the sentry in front of the chief official's house in each town, was merely a symbol of authority as in Europe, afterwards however, it becomes apparent that the system of Government in the Congo is based on absolute uniformity. Every Post, however big or small, has its State flag and every chief official, from the Governor to the chief of a Wood Post, has a sentry at his door. Each morning at sunrise the flag is hoisted, while the guard presents arms and every evening at sunset it is lowered with like ceremony. Indeed, the whole system is military, for everyone rises, works, eats and sleeps at the command of the clarion. It is a custom at most official and private parties in the Congo, to hand round port wine and cigars before sitting down to table. At first this seemed a strange kind of « aperative », but soon the glass of port became very agreeable after the morning's work.

Ten or twelve guests were assembled on the verandah when we arrived, and soon Mr. Armarni joined the group. He is an Italian, an ex-naval officer of distinction and now Commissaire du Roi of the Congo, a position which ranks with, but after, that of Governor General. By a simple and practical device, the relative rank of all the Administrative and Military officials can be determined at a glance.

Each wears a blue gauntlet on each wrist and forearm over the white sleeve of his coat and affixed on this are a number of gold bands. A captain of a river steamer, perhaps has three or four bands, a Chef de Poste, four or five, a Commissaire of a Zone or District, seven or eight, an Inspecteur d'Etat, nine or ten, and the Governor General, eleven. In order however, to economise space and perhaps to facilitate counting, when more than three stripes are worn, a broad strip is substituted which corresponds to the original three. Thus an official with five stripes wears one broad and two narrow ones, while the Governor General wears three broad stripes and two narrow ones. The chief decoration, the order of the Lion, can only be gained by Belgians, but the Congo Star is given to all after a certain term of service. Those who hold purely civil appointments such at Judges, Secretaries and Directors of Transport, wear no stripes at all.

At 2.30 p. m. a bugle sounded and a chattering throng of natives hurried past the Inspector's house towards the beach to resume work, which is always interrupted for three hours at 11.30 a. m. during the heat of the day. In order to feed these people and the soldiers of the Force Publique at Leopoldville, about a ton and a half of kwanga is prepared every day from the manioc grown in the villages around, and every able bodied native has to contribute his or her quota of work. Each person indeed is supposed to work for at least forty hours each month, and whether engaged on roads, buildings, or other public work, or in collecting rubber, wood for the steamers, or kwanga for food, is paid at the current rate. The principle of the system of Government, although entirely novel, is undoubtedly sound and suited to the country and the condition of the native. The whole territory is divided into two great parts, the lands of the native chiefs and the vacant lands called here the Domaine Privé. The Government has however, disposed of part of these to Concessionary Companies in this sense, that the Companies have the right to exploit all the products of the forest in these areas. Other portions have been leased to Missions, to Commercial Houses and to private people. The Government collects the rubber, ivory, food stuffs, and other produce from the Domain Lands and with the proceeds, constructs roads, navigates the rivers, maintains the Government and army and generally develops the country and civilises the natives.

Trading relations are formed with the chiefs as follows : Agents are sent into their districts with brass wire, cloth, salt, beads, or other things likely to attract the natives, and these are exchanged for rubber, ivory, gum copal, manioc, fish, fowl or other produce ; thus the value of rubber, ivory or any other substance is determined in terms of brass wire, cloth or salt and so its value in sterling. Similarly, the value of native labour is discovered and the native paid accordingly. The brass wire is cut into lengths called mitakos, this form of currency having been introduced by the late Sir H. M. Stanley. The length of the mitako, and so its value, varies in different parts of the country. At present there seems to be no limit to the amount of wire cut into mitakos, but as the natives use great quantities to make brass rings for the arms and legs of both sexes, it is difficult to say to what extent the currency is being debased. The pay of skilled labour here is high, and unskilled workers receive about as much as similar labourers in India. The natives pay no taxes in money or its equivalent, but instead are compelled to do this 40 hours' work per month for the State.

In the afternoon we cross the neck of Stanley Pool and visit Brazzaville, the capital of the French Congo. The town is situated close to the beach, but the Government offices are high up on a hill above. Having found the Secretariat, we explain that we are British travellers and desire to pay our respects to the Governor. The Secretary telephones as we wait in the office and presumably the Governor asks whether we have introductions and what we want, for the answer goes back *Non, ils sont venus, Pop!'!* However, the Governor, Mr. Gentil, who has spent many years in the Congo, receives us very kindly, offers to help us with steamers on the river, gives us some letters of introduction to French officials on the Ubangi and permits to shoot game. Every where indeed one meets with kindness, help and consideration from the officials in Africa, which is in marked contrast to the hide bound system of formalities which it is necessary to observe and maintain in Europe.

A great blowing of the steamer's whistle now takes place, for it is getting late and it is impossible to navigate the Congo after sunset. The captain is therefore becoming anxious, but enough light remains to see the buoys and we reach Leopoldville soon after 6 p. m. We have arranged to dine at the Mess, an excellent institution wherein all the Europeans of every rank, except the very highest officials, sit down together. The Commandant of the Force Publique, the Commandant of the Port, the Directors of

STEAMERS AND DOCKS AT LEOPOLDVILLE.

Transports and Posts, and the Doctors, all take their dinner with the working artisans. Altogether about 130 men attend the mess, where the cooking and service is excellent while each has a small bottle of wine and a cup of coffee. By this means, every man is ensured good wholesome food, and the necessity of restaurants, in which indiscriminate drinking might take place, is avoided.

Next morning, July 23rd. the *Flandre* leaves Leopoldville and steams to Kinshasa where we stop and land. Here as usual the keynote is development. Roads are being made, avenues of palms, mangoes and pine apples planted and store houses, factories and plantations constructed. At the coffee factory here, the beans are extracted from the shells, sorted into sizes and qualities and packed in bags. Many kinds of coffee have been planted in the Congo, but none are equal to the wild variety found in the forest, which is as good as any in the world when properly made. Near at hand is a brick field, where the bricks are made in metal moulds, the clay being forced in by long levers. They are not made as quickly as those fashioned by a machine but the process is a great improvement on the old-fashioned method of brick making in wooden moulds. It is already apparent that beer is regarded as a luxury here so we order some dozens at three francs a bottle and having taken some photos return to the ship.

On the beach were some fine elephant tusks which have been collected by the agents of the *Société Anonyme Belge*. When a native finds a pair of tusks in the territory of the company, the State takes one as a royalty and the company buys the other for a certain quantity of cloth. This only represents a fraction of the value in Europe, but is gladly

4

accepted by the native who has no use for it except to make war horns. Indeed in the old days, the chiefs used to form a kind of fence round their huts by sticking the points in the ground, little thinking that in another part of the world, not even the millionaire of fiction ever constructed such an expensive railing. Then the Arab slave raiders came and stole both the native women and the ivory, so that the white man who gives beautiful coloured cloth for these useless elephants' tusks is regarded as a very generous trader. In the afternoon the *Flandre* continued her journey threading her way between the numerous islands in Stanley Pool, and finally tied up to the bank of the island of Bamu which is French territory. This island enjoys the distinction of being the only one in the Congo which has an owner, for all the rest are declared to be no man's land by international treaty. It is reputed to be full of game, and we go ashore to look for it, but return without seeing anything. As the mosquitoes prevent all sleep in the cabin, we arrange to make up a bed on deck and obtain a better night's rest, for it is comparatively cool here in the evening in the open.

I am very anxious to bathe next morning, but the captain strongly disadvises for the currents are very strong here, and the river is full of crocodiles. In the midst of breakfast we are startled by the report that the ship is on fire, and smoke is seen to be issuing from the fore hatch, under which much of the wood used for fuel is stored. None of the Europeans however, are more excited than the natives, who, leisurely and with due deliberation, hand up buckets of water. Nothing indeed could make a native hurry. The captain seems a trifle upset, and states that it

may be necessary to run on a rock, and thus make a hole
in the bows and flood the hold.   This seems to be rather
a desperate remedy, but no one shows the slightest interest.   This appeared curious at the time ; sinće however,
it has transpired that fires in the holds are of common
occurrence, and that as the ships are all of iron, they
usually burn themselves out without harming anything.
Soon after however, the captain with an alarmed look,
rushes up on deck and said that a terrible crime or a great
mistake had been committed.   It appeared that by some
error, our cases of beer and some others belonging to
Commandant Sillye had been left on the beach at Kinshasa.
Immediately we anchored last night a native boatswain,
or capita, was sent with six men in a canoe to fetch
them and ought to have returned by midnight.   Nothing
however, was heard of the boat until now when the capita
appeared and told a harrowing story.   He found the cases
all right and started to return across the river, but as it
began to blow hard, he thought it better to make for land
and wait until the morning before trying to find the ship.
He succeeded in landing on the island of Bamu and soon
after a white man appeared with some Senegalese soldiers
and demanded to know what was in the cases.   He
explained, when the white man fired and killed all the
crew, but he ran away and escaped.   The affair seemed
serious so Lord Mountmorres and Commandant Sillye left for
Brazzaville to discover the truth, while I stayed on the ship
to superintend the landing of our cargo if the fire extended.

Soon after the Commandant of the Port of Leopoldville
arrived in a steamer and asked if we wanted assistance as
another ship had run on the rocks higher up and sunk and

he was hastening to rescue any possible survivors.   Sunday, July 24th indeed, seemed to be a veritable day of horrors, but still no one appeared at all excited.   By midday the fire in the forehold was extinguished and thus one danger was removed.   Later in the afternoon just before sunset, an immense flock of ducks and geese crossed the river, but as they were flying nearly a hundred feet up in the air, it was impossible to shoot them. Soon after Mountmorres and Sillye returned and reported they had found all the crew safe, except one man who had probably deserted and had also brought back the cases of beer.   The white man was a French officer of Customs, who had naturally thought the crew of the canoe were engaged in smuggling and had fired blank cartridges to frighten them.   So passed an eventful day with much smoke but little fire.   It was indeed becoming apparent that the Congo was a true land of exaggerations. On all sides were great hills, great plains, great forests, great rivers, great beasts, great trees, and great lies.

Next day we continued our course up Stanley-Pool, which meant threading our way up narrow channels between uninteresting sandbanks covered with forest or grass.   In the distance could be seen the hills forming the boundaries of the Pool and at its upper end *Dover Cliffs* so called from their resemblance to that part of the English coast.   About midday we sighted the *Anversville,* the vessel which was supposed to have been sunk, comfortably lying on a sand bank, and the *Brugesville* which had gone to her assistance, also resting on the same bank. One of the passengers came off to the *Flandre* and told us that no one was hurt and all the baggage was safe and that

he had heard we had been burnt out, attacked by natives
and all killed. Truly the Congo is a wonderful place.

As the *Flandre* moors we decide to go ashore hunting.
Within a few yards of the bank is the lair of a hippopo-
tamus and the spoor of elephants. It is however, very
difficult walking, for patches of land are covered with long
grass seven or eight feet high and the rest is bog. After
struggling along for a few minutes, I hear a curious noise
like a very asthmatic fog horn not above five yards away.
Nothing is however, visible, for the grass forms a complete cover. Again the grunt with a suspicious after-
sniff and at the same moment Chikaia, who is carrying
my gun snaps his fingers— the usual sign to indicate game
—and beckons me to follow. I endeavour to do so, and
at once sink in the bog up to the knees, but fortunately
keep my rifle dry. By clutching the grass, I get out and
we follow the spoor of the hippo as rapidly as possible.
This is very clearly marked, for the grass has been recently
thrust aside and there are great holes in the soft mud over
a foot wide and deep, made by the great feet of the beast.
These holes were in pairs lying close together, showing
that the hippo was galloping as he passed and unfortunately they led straight to the river.

Next day we leave the Pool and enter a part of the river
called the Channel. Here there are no islands and both
banks are visible all the time, the width not being more
than a mile in some places. A low range of hills covered
with acacias or coarse grass, exists on each side. As
usual, we stop at a Wood Post to take fuel on board.
This is cut in logs three or four feet long and stacked in
heaps about the same in width and height. Sticks are

placed in the ground connected by lines at the required height and the logs are laid in rows until the space is filled. The result is a cubic yard of wood known in the Congo as a *bras*, but the bras differs in size and price considerably, in some cases the cost being 5 mitakos and in others double that amount. A native can easily collect a bras of wood in the forest and carry it to the bank in a day and in some of the Wood Posts fifty or sixty natives are employed. Even then however, the demand for wood by the big steamers is sometimes greater than the supply.

At 6 p. m. every day the steamer stops for the night and makes fast to a tree on the bank. All the native passengers at once go ashore, light fires and arrange their beds for the night. They sleep on mats or with the whole body, and head also, wrapped up closely in rugs. Either their feet or heads are always within a few inches of the fire and their bodies radiate out like the spokes of a wheel. Until 9 30 p. m , however, when all lights on the steamer must be put out, a ceaseless chatter proceeds with an occasional angry discussion as the natives take their meal of kwanga, fish, and any odd piece of meat they can procure. It is a somewhat weird sight, the black forms showing dimly in the ruddy light of the fires under the trees. The bell on the steamer rings the command and everyone goes to bed, and then one appreciates the real silence of the equatorial forest which one has heard about at home. Within a few yards, hundreds of frogs commence to croak loudly and continue steadily, with a few pauses to breathe, until daybreak. Hundreds of monkeys screech shrilly in the trees and millions of mosquitoes hum steadily within an inch or two of one's ears. All manner of animal cries

THE AMERICAN MISSION HOUSE AT LEOPOLDVILLE.

are heard in the forest and the hippos blow loudly as they
rise to, the surface to breathe.   As a matter of fact, the
noise at midnight in the forest, when every beast, bird and
insect is busy hunting for food, is greater than at any other
time, and at midday only, one enjoys comparative quiet
when all the animal kingdom is asleep.

One evening I went ashore with Chikaia for a stroll on
the beach, carrying only a gun. We soon found a number
of ducks and as they had never been fired at before probably, they were not scared away by the noise of the gun,
but kept wheeling round and round overhead affording
very easy shots.   It would indeed have been easy to shoot
them all.   There was, however, no reason to do so and
having collected a couple or two to make a welcome change
from the daily goat of the steamer, we started back when
a fine antelope-cheval rushed from the wood across the
sandy beach towards the water.   Chikaia at once became
very excited and wished me to fire, but it was useless, as
the beast was more than a hundred yards away.   It was
satisfactory to find the boy was a keen sportsman, even
though he did not appreciate the different capacities of
a gun and a rifle.   However, I made a mental note never
to go, even for a casual stroll in Africa, without both
weapons.

On returning to the ship, we hear that the Captain's boy
has killed a hippo and that dozens of others are waiting
to be shot.   We therefore determine to try some shooting
by moonlight and Chikaia is delighted when he sees the
gras as he calls my Lee-Metford come out of its case.
It is a beautiful night with clear, cool air.   Streams of
silver flow from the moon on the water, while the palms

tower high with majestic crowns.   Here we are in the very
midst of real nature and yet again it unpleasantly recalls
the scenery of a theatre.   It is indeed extraordinary with
what accuracy scenic artists construct tropical scenes.
The surroundings tend to make one sentimental and regret
that this veritable garden of Eden should be exploited to
make billiard balls and rubber tyres for automobiles and
bicycles.   The native also, instead of hunting elephant
and hippos, eating his fill and sleeping, and eating again
and sleeping again until the carcase has disappeared and
then hunting again, now has to collect rubber juice and
cut wood for an ugly looking steam flat.   Such however,
is civilisation in the Congo.

Spoor of elephants and hippos abound and the grunt of
the latter can frequently be heard, but they are not sitting
up on their haunches waiting to be shot.   The clear,
shrill chirp of the sentry bird is indeed warning the big
beasts that something strange is moving and we shall have
to lie still for a long while probably before getting a chance
at the great heads as they are raised from the water.

After a walk of about a mile, we arrive at the place
where the captain's boy was supposed to have killed the
hippo.   The truth was he had *fired at* a beast who, as the
spoor clearly showed, had walked calmly into the river and
not a trace of blood could be seen.   After a time, with
practice perhaps, one will be able to gauge the truth from
an ordinary Congo statement.

Next day we reach the mouth of the Kasai, a large tri-
butary which drains much of the Equatorial District of the
Congo.   Here is a State Post, Kwamouth, with a few well
constructed houses and a Catholic Mission where pretty

walking sticks with ivory handles can be purchased and
where the Fathers make a few cigars from Congo tobacco
which are not at all bad smoking.   A little further up the
river, is the deserted Catholic Mission of St. Marie which
has evidently been at one time well arranged with a large
manioc plantation and garden.   Here however, the
Sleeping Sickness appeared and the mortality was so heavy
that the place was abandoned.   The disease had no doubt
existed before, but it was this terrible epidemic which first
attracted the serious notice of Europeans.

It is becoming clear that there are a great number of
nationalities represented in the Congo.   Most of the political and military appointments are held by Belgians, but
there are many Italian military officers also.   Nearly all
the marine are Scandinavians and the language of the river
is therefore, chiefly English, although every State official
must speak a certain amount of French.   A few Germans
also hold appointments, and the trading houses are run
chiefly by English and Dutch, while there are missionaries
of several nationalities.   In the army, orders are given
in French, but on the ships and in the stations, the native
is commanded in a kind of jargon based on the Bangala
dialect.   The Danish captain of a Congo steamer thus as a
rule, speaks, besides his own language, English, French
and Bangala and can make himself understood in all.

On pay day, rolls of brass wire are cut up into mitakos,
which become longer the higher one travels up the river,
this arrangement having been introduced by Stanley and
never altered.   Here the mitako is 28 centimetres long and
it is worth 5 cents, while at Basoko it is 40 centimetres
long and worth 10 cents.   The native crew are paid three

mitakos for their food per day which would purchase twice
as much kwanga as they could possibly eat.   The capitas
and wheelman are also paid monthly wages which vary with
the nature of their work.

By July 28th we have passed through the Channel into
a portion of the river which is very wide and has the appearance of a great lake studded with islands.   The banks
are invisible, for the country here is absolutely flat and
continues so for many hundreds of miles until the Province
Orientale is reached.   Between these islands, which are
usually well wooded, we pass slowly up the river, for the
current is still strong although the surface of the water
appears absolutely still and the light glares as from a
mirror.   Some of the islands are however, only covered
with grass and a herd of buffaloes on one come charging
down to the river to drink.   Unfortunately one of the passengers fires a kind of saloon rifle, which might possibly
have killed a rabbit at twenty yards, and frightens them
back.   This is a great pity, for if we had had time, we
could easily have bagged one or two and had some fresh
beef for dinner.

At midday on the 29th we reach Mopolenga and stop
for wood.   The land in the neighbourhood is well cultivated and manioc, sweet potatoes, bananas and pineapples
flourish.   The manioc plant has a green stem, reddish
branches and green leaves arranged in clusters of six
which turn downwards forming the shape of a parasol,
evidently a popular, as it is an appropriate, pattern for
vegetable life in this hot country.   The root of the manioc
yields the flour, which is made into kwanga and unless it
is well boiled, is supposed to be very injurious.   The

animals here consist chiefly of monkeys, parrots and finches, but many ducks fly from a swamp near the water.

In the afternoon we reach Bolobo, the head quarters of the Baptist Mission, which is presided over by Mr. Grenfell, a missionary who has resided for over twenty years in the Congo. He has taught the natives to make bricks and build houses and has erected a Mission Hall, a hospital and a printing house. The mission enclosure is well laid out with mango trees and other useful fruits and many fat ducks and fowls pass a contented existence there. Unfortunately Mr. Grenfell was not at home, but we were fortunate in finding Mr. Scrivener, another missionary, who has resided some years in Africa. He stated that the natives were emigrating from the District of Lake Leopold, which lies behind Bolobo and is Domain Land, because they were forced to collect rubber and were flogged if they refused. He had never himself seen a native who had been ill treated, but had been told so by natives. Asked whether the people were ever mutilated, Mr. Scrivener looked very surprised and answered « Oh no, there is nothing of that kind now! »

Bolobo is very populous and many natives flocked down to the beach immediately the steamer arrived and at once held an outdoor market on the beach selling manioc, fish, clothes, pots of various kinds and other articles to the crew and passengers. A Congo flat fish of the perch family is found here, smoke dried and sold for food and is very good eating indeed.

Two of the crew were « chicotted » to-day by order of the captain. One had attacked another boy with a knife and wounded him and the other had stolen, and then falsely blamed another. The *chicotte* is a plain strip of hippo hide and the punishment was administered publicly by the capita on the bridge of the steamer and did not appear to be more painful than an ordinary birching at a public school.

At 10 p. m. we decide to take the big iron boat of the steamer and go hunting. The natives are exceedingly skilful and know all the likely places for hippo. They first paddle hard up stream and having arrived at the hunting ground allow the boat to drift down with the current in perfect silence. It is clear moonlight, but it is necessary to cover the fore sight of the rifle with white paper in order to see it clearly. After a time, up rises a great head with a great pant and there is just time for a shot before it sinks again. Hippos frequent shallow water and are indifferent swimmers. They walk about on the bottom and rise at intervals to breathe. It is thus impossible to know in which direction a beast will next appear or whether he will come up under the boat and capsize it. This night there were great numbers and we had excellent sport. One shot in the head is sufficient to kill a hippo which then sinks and the body does not rise again for some hours. One unfortunate animal was however, shot in the back and rearing straight up on his hind legs rushed for some yards in that attitude until a second shot in the head put him out of his misery.

Next day we reach Lukolela, a Wood Post and telegraph station. The line runs along the bank all the way from Leopoldville to Coquilhatville and was very difficult to erect. A space had to be cleared in the forest nearly two hundred feet wide and the line erected in the centre on iron posts, so that any falling trees would not destroy it. At first, the elephants strongly resented these novel posts and frequently knocked them down as easily as if they had been nine pins, but have since become used to them. At Lukolela there is excellent teak wood which is fashioned into doors and windows and shipped to various places ready for building. The nights are quite cool, although we are near the Equator and the heat in the day time is not nearly as oppresive as it is at Aden or Shanghai in the summer. Cultivation is much more advanced here than in the lower Congo and the physique of the natives is remarkably fine.

The navigation of the river here becomes very difficult, for the water is shallow at this season of the year and there are many sand banks which frequently change their position. Charts are therefore, practically useless and each skipper has to feel his way each voyage. Indeed, the whole time two boys sit on the bows of the vessel with long poles sounding the water and shouting out the depth. It is curious that when the vessel is travelling in shallow water, the engines at once go slow of their own accord. One of the engineers explained that this phenomena was produced by the difficulty the wheels experienced in dragging away, so to speak, the water from under the ship when there was little depth. Still the ships, frequently run on the banks, but as they are flat bottomed, are not usually injured. The method of mooring is very rudimentary although practical. One of the crew jumps overboard with a steel rope, swims ashore and makes it fast to a tree. All of them are expert swimmers and seem to enjoy their frequent dips, and as their clothes consist of a loin cloth only, they do not require to undress.

On August 1st at sunset we reach Irebu, an exceedingly beautiful place. An avenue of palms stretches parallel to the river and about twenty yards from it the bank itself being fenced by white wooden rails. This leads to a large open square around which are the brick houses of the European officers. Beyond, along the river front, are more brick houses, the Mess and the Magazines, and gardens are laid out the whole length of the town. This is one of the large military training centres, where about a dozen officers prepare more than a thousand recruits for the Force Publique.

In the evening the place was illuminated by very simple, but effective, means. Stakes were driven into the ground and on each was placed a tin which presumably had contained condensed milk. These were filled with palm oil and pieces of wood to serve as wicks. The mosquitoes here are very bad indeed and it is necessary to take quinine every day to counteract the effects of their poison.

At daybreak next morning most of the troops were exercising in the square and their precision and manœuvring were really marvellous. Any European colonel might indeed be proud to hear such a single click as his regiment shouldered arms. The officers state that the natives attend very carefully all the time for the word of command and act very quickly after it is given. The native corporals evidently make good instructors and the raw recruit is soon converted into a smart and responsible soldier. This military education is certainly the best that could be given to a savage; it teaches him punctuality, regularity, obedience and collective responsibility; it shows him how to build houses and keep them clean and it gives him an idea of

justice for he knows he will be punished for wrong doing.
The soldier therefore soon becomes an altogether different
person and realises that he is no longer an animal-man
living wild in the forest, but a soldier-man and a friend
of the great « Bulamatadi » who governs the country.
What we may call the caste feeling has indeed contributed
greatly to civilising the country. Anyone who is brought
into direct contact with the whites as a soldier, a worker
in the plantation or on the roads, soon feels that he is
superior to the wild bushman and then becomes more
attached to his new master than to his own cousins. It is
rather amusing to hear the native domestics or « boys »
who probably rank higher than any other natives on the
social ladder, speaking of the « indigenes » with great
contempt as though they were quite another and an infe-
rior species. Speaking of « Bulamatadi, » it may be of
interest to state the origin and meaning of the term—it
means literally in the native tongue « one who breaks
stones » and was given to Stanley, when he blasted rocks
to make roads the term being afterwards buried with him
on his coffin. Since then it has been applied to all officials
of the State and is used to connote anything and everything connected with the State. Thus the State side of the
river is Bulamatadi, a State Post is Bulamatadi, a State
steamer is Bulamatadi, anything indeed belonging to the
State is Bulamatadi. White men traders and hunters, not
State officials, are « mundellas, » but the native at once
has a nick name for everyone which describes his chief
characteristic. Lord Mountmorres usually wore long
hunting boots and was named « big boots » and as I
wore eyeglasses, I became « double eyes. »

We left Irebu on August 2nd and at once disturbed many crocodiles and hippos, which abound in this district. An unfortunate accident happened in the afternoon. One of the crew fell overboard and must have been drawn under the stern wheel and struck by a paddle, for he never re-appeared and no sign of the poor fellow could be found, although diligent search was made for a long time.

Just before sunset a canoe comes alongside and fastens to the ship, although it is travelling at full speed. It is indeed wonderful to see the way the natives manipulate these narrow dug-outs not two feet wide. In this one were three fishermen with some fish which looked like trout for sale. At once a great clamouring takes place among the native passengers and it soon becomes plain that the chief fisherman was a good man of business. Having taken an empty bottle for one fish and a piece of cloth for another, he refused more of those articles and demanded either salt or mitakos for his goods. In a short time however, he had disposed of his cargo and paddled contentedly away.

The natives are very vain and take much trouble over their personal appearance. As their clothes are very simple this is concentrated on their tatouage and on their hair dressing. From a hopeless looking tangle of black tow a very pretty erection is created by the barbers who are of both sexes. Often the hair has five or six separate partings and quills or feathers are inserted into the ridges in between. All the women here wear a simple piece of cloth as they do in the Lower Congo and sometimes a plain leather belt is worn round the waist. The arms and legs are bare and covered with plain bangles made of mitakos. The women wear no hat of any kind, but the men ape the

NATIVES OF THE UPPER CONGO.

Europeans and appear in old helmets or straw hats.   Both
sexes are very clean personally, and bathe frequently in
the river, but never dry themselves afterwards.   The men
keep on their loin cloths, but if they wear also shirts or
trousers, take these off, while the women bathe in a white
linen loin cloth and everyone afterwards pulls on his other
clothes without drying.   Many natives rub a red powder
into the skin made from cam-wood and thus acquire a
copper colour, while others paint their faces with various
stripes of red, yellow or white.   On the Congo however,
where the natives are becoming civilised, this custom seems
to be dying out.

On August 3rd we cross the Equator marked by a post
on one side of the river and the point of an island in the
centre.   Here used to be a settlement, but most of the
people have moved higher up.   There is still a Mission
near the place and a good road runs along the bank
between plantations of bananas and gardens to Coquilhatville which we reach in the afternoon.

BOTANICAL GARDENS AT EALA.

CHAPTER IV.

The Equator District.

Coquilhatville, the capital of this important District is the largest town in the Upper Congo. The roads are formed by bamboos laid in rows, upon which sand and mud are placed the whole forming an effective pavement for foot passengers and no other is required for there are no carriages and only a few horses. All the officers don white uniforms with full dress, badges and medals, and together we proceed to make a formal call on Captain Stevens, the Commissaire of the District with whom is staying Mr. Malfeyt, Commissaire du Roi. Some of the officers take their dogs with them, which at once make a furious onslaught on the numerous cats of the Commissaire and have to be suppressed.   Mgr. Derikx places a particularly pugnacious fox-terrier under the basket work of his chair the little animal being literally sat upon by the dignitary of the Church.

The Residency is a large brick building situated on a low hill and raised above the ground, the space beneath being enclosed and loop-holed, thus forming a small fort. The gardens are particularly pretty and well kept.   Beer is handed round and we sit chatting on the verandah until Mr. Grenfell, the head of the Baptist Mission, arrives.   He has travelled up the river in the Mission Steamer from Bolobo and was on his way when we stopped at that place. As he has been in the Congo for more than twenty years, he knows the country well and thus speaks with authority. He thinks the system of Government excellent, but that it is administered better in the Lower than the Upper Congo, because there are not enough officials in the latter.   He is convinced the population has greatly decreased on the riverside of the Bangala District, and attributes it chiefly to Sleeping Sickness for he cannot say if emigration to the French Congo has been extensive or not.   No case of ill-treatment of natives has come to his notice during the last three years, but he thinks the State does not give them enough work to do.   He has seen natives without hands, but does not believe that any atrocities have occurred for many years.   Generally speaking, he thinks it would be better if the State acquired all the property of the Companies.   Although he does not know of any definite cases of ill-treatment, he has heard reports and thinks there is « no smoke without fire. » However, he is quite prepared to agree that a very little fire in the Congo makes a great deal of smoke. Altogether, Mr. Grenfell spoke very calmly, and is evidently not carried away by emotionalism or strong prejudice against the State.

At Coquilhatville, as elsewhere in the State, the prisoners are given useful work to do. Near by a party were digging a hole by the roadway. They were chained together but the chain was so long that it did not hamper their movements. Two policemen were on guard, but the whole gang were evidently taking matters very easily.

In the evening we dine with the Commissaire and a party of sixteen or eighteen, including many of our fellow travellers, Mr. Grenfell and Dr. Dutton, of the Liverpool School of Tropical Medicine, who is here studying the Sleeping Sickness. Everyone we meet who has travelled in other countries and also visited the Congo, is astonished at the wonderful development of the place. It is indeed becoming more and more apparent that the State has gone ahead very fast and that the stress has been great, both for Europeans and natives. Probably, now the machine is fairly set rolling, it will proceed more steadily in the future.

Next day we decide to leave the *Flandre* and stay for a week or so at Coquilhatville. Commandant Ankström, the Adjoint Superieur to the Commissaire, kindly lends us his house and we at once move in, glad to leave the mosquitoes of the river and to sleep in a room once more. Everything in the house and garden is scrupulously clean and tidy, characteristics which I may add were found in nearly every Post and house in the whole country. The sanitary arrangements are the perfection of simplicity. There are no drains, but simple receptables which are emptied and cleaned every morning while carbolic acid is used liberally.   This admirable system is carried out in every Post, however large or small, and I never once found it unobserved.   The natives themselves are also very cleanly in their habits, so that although the heat is great and decomposition proceeds very rapidly, bad smells are absolutely unknown.   Near the residency is a well kept farm and the mutton tasted particularly nice after the diet of goat on the steamer.

The effect of the climate on my digestion is curious. In Europe all forms of starch and sugar give me indigestion and I have therefore to avoid bread, potatoes, jam, sugar and kindred substances.   Here however, I have a craving for these things and never have indigestion.   I mention this personal trait, because many other travellers in the tropics have often stated that they could march on rice and jam for days without desiring meat of any kind. No doubt the system is working at, so to speak, high pressure, but it is curious that a complete change in one's idiosyncrasies should take place even in the first month.

On August 5th the *Flandre* proceeds up the river, and we bid farewell to our travelling companions, who seem to have become old friends in the last six weeks.   Everyone, is always most kind and courteous, and not only gives every information, but also the benefit of his experience, and thus affords much valuable assistance.   The town of Coquilhatville consists of rows of brick houses standing in their own gardens and fronting on avenues. It may seem that one insists unnecessarily on the fact that the houses are brick in all the towns, a fact which the European would accept as a matter of course. The traveller however knows that in most tropical countries, wood is usually employed instead, as being easier to obtain and work. Indeed in the United States, the country seats of even the very wealthy are generally constructed chiefly of that substance. Bricks however, are by no means easily made in the Congo, for in many places the soil is very sandy and it is therefore difficult to make the brick bind. Again, lime is very scarce and all manner of substances are used to make mortar. Among these the ant hills are much in favour, for it has been observed that these structures which are often thirty feet high and in proportion great in diameter, never disintegrate in the heaviest rain. When dug out and mixed with sand their substance makes an excellent mortar. Again, the shells of oysters, which abound in some parts of the river are also used to make mortar with good results. The roofs are thatched with palm leaves wherever obtainable, and if well constructed are quite water tight. Glass windows are not much used, for as much air as possible is desirable and the verandahs are so broad that rain rarely enters. The openings are thus closed only by shutters or by wire gauze to keep out the numerous insects.

Living here is very expensive. The usual money is the mitako, but the native likes salt and will sometimes take cloth if he fancies it. He is however, very independent, and on one occasion a native refused 14/- in cloth for a single duck. Fowls and eggs are about the same price as in the West End of London, but the latter are very scarce. Fruit is however, cheap, as it is abundant. Near the town is a large coffee and cocoa plantation arranged in square fields, separated by avenues of palms, which both form grateful shade and yield much palm oil. On each field is a large board on which is painted the number of bushes. Papye, cœur de bœuf, bananas and pineapples abound.

The system of work in every Post is exactly the same, so that a description of it as witnessed in Coquilhatville would equally do for every place in the Congo. At 5.30 a. m. reveille and at 6 a. m. roll call of all the Europeans and native workers who then, led by a bugler, march off to their respective duties. At 11.15 a. m. bugle call and all the natives march to the river and bathe. Al 11.30 a. m. bathing ceases and they march off behind the bugler to dinner and rest. At 2.30 p. m. they assemble again and at 5.30 p. m. finish for the day. The native thus works eight hours and a half and rests in the hottest portion of the day. The workers in the plantations are entirely volunteers and so do not come under the 40 hours' rule, which is only applied to those who live in the villages and are not in the State service. The women do the light work in the plantations and thus fare much better, than when forced to do all the work by their husbands, which happens in all the villages. It is curious to see them brushing the roads with palm leaves. Six or eight women walk abreast and push away the dust and dead leaves which are then collected in baskets and thrown into the river.

As our house looks into the square where the Force Publique drill, we witness the methods employed. At first the recruit is taught which is right and which is left.

Droite and up goes the right hand, *gauche* and the left follows. The native corporal, however, has corrupted these words into *hi hoo* so that, as is usual in military commands, no mere civilian can possibly understand them. Afterwards when he comes to mount guard and relieve sentries, the order *présentez armes!* might be anything from the sound.

The band practices also close at hand. First the cornet picks out some air he has heard, note by note, and like a child who is learning the piano, always goes back to the beginning of the piece when he strikes a false note. After many trials the whole air is discovered. Then the trombones and bass instruments put in the accompaniment also by experiment, and in the end the result is really quite good for Africans unlike Asiatics, take kindly to European music.

The method of moving heavy weights is necessarily very primitive, for, with the exception of a few wheel-barrows, there are no vehicles of any kind here. A huge tree trunk was carried into the square one day; pieces of wood had been lashed across it about two feet apart throughout its length. One or two men on each side of each piece then lifted it and the whole eighty or hundred men marched the trunk along with ease at a jog trot. It would indeed be impossible to use heavy trolleys in this part of the Congo, for the roads are sandy and the wheels would at once sink deeply into them.

A walk through the plantation, which extends over some square miles, is very pleasant, as the palms spread their leaves across the avenues until they nearly touch each other thus forming beautiful shady groves. Ferns grow round the stems and the whole is extremely pretty and cool-looking.   Beyond the plantation is the cemetery for the whites.   Each grave is covered with bricks and has a wooden cross at the head on which is inscribed the name and date of death.   The age however, is omitted and this is perhaps as well, for the Congo exacts a heavy toll of young lives and new comers are often depressed already by the accounts of the climate which have reached Europe.

Further on is a forest through which runs a narrow native tract.   This demonstrates well the extreme indolence of the native.   If a small branch of a tree falls across the path, he steps over it, if a large one, he walks round it.   Time is no object, so the length of the road is immaterial.   No attempt is made to form bridges, for the streams are not deep and are easily fordable, nor even to break off the branches of trees which obstruct the way.   It is easier to stoop and pass beneath.   The forest paths have indeed been made simply by the pressure of bare feet on the soil and undergrowth.   A few monkeys and parrots chatter overhead and an occasional pigeon coos, but the chief forms of animal life here, are thousands of the most lovely butterflies.   These are coloured to suit the surroundings and are therefore usually of subdued tints. Occasionally however, a great insect nearly as large as one's hand, flies by exhibiting the most vivid greens, reds, and blues.   Bananas, rubber plants, palms and acacias crowd each other in the forest through which we walk for three or four miles, until we reach a native village consisting of a few square huts in a clearing.   A handsome looking fellow comes up to us, salutes and desires to know if we wish to buy anything.   Having neither mitakos, salt, nor cloth except the pyjamas we are wearing, we cannot deal and leave the man wondering probably — if the native ever does wonder — why we walked all that distance if we did not require anything.

On August 8th we visit the Botanical Gardens at Eala, which is about three miles from Coquilhatville. Mr. Pinard, the Director of the Gardens, shows us the various plants indigenous and imported which he has collected, and although the place has only been formed for three years, almost everything which could possibly grow has been planted. The soil is sandy, the altitude about 1100 feet above sea level and the temperature is about 90° F. Numerous varieties of rubber plants are arranged here for experimental purposes, and gutta percha also is slowly attaining maturity. Bushes which yield acid, suitable for coagulating the milk of the rubber plant, grow alongside. Cotton does not do well here owing to the scarcity of rain, but coffee and tea flourish. All the palms, many ferns and orchids and nearly every fruit and vegetable, European as well as tropical, grow in great profusion while the melons, vegetable marrows, beans, peas, potatoes, lettuces, cucumbers and tomatoes look healthy. Croton, belladonna and other medicinal herbs are cultivated and there are many beautiful flowers, whose use is chiefly ornamental. The gardens are of great extent, well laid out and beautifully kept, so that it is difficult to believe that four years ago this site was wild forest.

Adjoining the gardens is a large farm in which cattle, resembling those of the Lower Congo, look well. It is however, unfortunate that the cows only give sufficient milk to rear their calves. Horses, asses and pigs live healthily and the native sheep thrive, but are very thin.   Although wheat will not grow, maize is easily raised and the grass, if coarse looking, is good for grazing.   The farm buildings are kept most scrupulously clean, for the slightest neglect would probably occasion an epidemic of trichinosis among the pigs.

The villages in the neighbourhood of Coquilhatville seem very populous and prosperous.   Any morning early whole families can be met—father, mother and children, with bundles of manioc fastened on their backs by broad grass fibres—going to the town.   Everywhere the natives seem contented and happy.   When not working, they sit in the roads and dye their skins or have their hair dressed, while the children play around with bows and arrows or other pugnacious kind of toys.   The wealthy wear heavy brass rings extending from the ankle to the knee and the discomfort must be very great, but as is proved by the tatouage, the natives will bear much pain in order to beautify themselves.   Before leaving Coquilhatville, we send for the boy Epondo, who was rendered famous as an example of an atrocity by Mr. Casement, the late British Consul at Boma. Epondo is now employed as a gardener by the Commissaire of the District and is always at hand when visitors desire to see him.   Four inches below the elbow joint of the left arm there are two deeps scars, three inches apart, which could certainly have been produced by the bite of an animal of about the size of a wild boar.   The stump of the forearm is covered with irregular scars, such as would remain if the hand had become gangrenous and fallen away. It was useless asking him questions, as he had already told two distinct stories which have been related above.

On August 10th. we leave Coquilhatville and steam down the river to Irebu, which we reach after a few hours hot journey. Mr. Jeniaux, the Commandant, has spared no pains to make the camp not only beautiful but attractive in every way and it has well earned its reputation as one of the show places of the Congo. Lord Mountmorres is lodged in a spare house used for guests and Lieutenant Hoyer kindly lends me his during our stay. The Mess is very comfortably arranged, and the dinner based on antelope and wild pig is excellent.

Next day I go hunting with Mr. Hoyer in a canoe propelled by twenty paddlers. These at first keep up a kind of chant to the time of the paddles which is quite musical and pleasant. As we approach the game grounds however, they become quite silent. After travelling up stream for about a mile, we land in a kind of bog which is full of a species of duck, somewhat resembling a wood-cock. A sergeant of the Force Publique acts as guide and hunter, and it soon becomes apparent that the native is in the habit of stalking even birds and shooting them sitting. This is natural enough for formerly they were armed with bows and arrows, and now the army of course use only rifles. Shot guns, therefore, are only known to the boys of the white men, some of whom are very good shots. The hunter seems quite annoyed because I only shoot at birds on the wing, but is delighted when one falls. So far indeed, the only enthusiasm a native has shown, has been while hunting after a successful shot. The paddlers at once re-enact the scene, put imaginary guns to their shoulders give a loud bang and then describe circles with their hands to give a dumb show of the bird falling, laughing and shouting all the time.   They are realy just like young children and are easily pleased by trifles. After walking some distance the sergeant becomes wildly excited and clutches me violently by the arm but makes no noise.   Looking up I see a large monkey but signify that I will not shoot those beasts.   He then asks permission to fire his rifle and brings it down with a shot through the head.   After this we paddle on to the hippo ground. After the very first shot at a head fifty yards away, the canoe suddenly gives a great lurch and as nearly as possible capsizes.   Another great beast had evidently chosen that moment to come up just under it and if we had not been a heavy load, would undoubtedly have thrown it high in the air.   As it was, beyond a shaking, no one was damaged and we had excellent sport for a few minutes until the animals made for the bank and hid themselves in the long grass.

Behind Irebu is a plain, where the grass is really green, the green that is only seen in the tropics.   Here and there are clumps of palms and patches of forest, the whole giving the appearance of a well kept park.   There are antelope and wild pig here but they are very difficult to stalk owing to the open character of the ground.   There are also a few red-legged partridges and many pigeons so that one always found something to shoot.

The native camp here consists of a large square shut off by a wooden fence.   Inside are large huts in which the soldiers live, and oddly enough, they all prefer to have separate establishments, each woman preparing the food for her husband.   These women also work in the plantation when they are not concerned with the business of maternity, which judging by the number of children about, must be very seldom. The native cemetery is a curious-looking place, for on each grave is placed the clothes of the dead one and any other belongings he has. No one knows the origin or object of this custom They are not for the journey to the happy hunting ground apparently, for missionaries say they have never heard the natives speak of any kind of a future state. It may be that these articles are merely to show the wealth of the departed; they are however, all broken or torn to shreds, so that no robber should be tempted to take them. Many of the tribes are said to eat their dead, except those of high position and those who die of infectious diseases, and others used to throw the corpses in the river. Some tribes however, have a very elaborate funeral with much wailing and lamenting and the departed is interred beneath his own hut, which is never occupied again.

At Irebu, the narrow river from Lake Tumba joins the Congo, and from its small size is known usually as the canal. The current sometimes flows up and sometimes down, according to the height of water in the Congo, but it is obvious that the general direction must be down, as many small streams flow into the Lake, and all their water is certainly not dispersed by evaporation. Many crocodiles pass up and down the canal and it would be easy to shoot them from the windows or verandah of my house, but it seems to be rather a waste of cartridges which, like most other things, must be carried the whole tour, for none can be procured in the Congo. I do not therefore, care to run the risk of running short when the hunting grounds of Uele are reached.

Sunday is usually a very busy day in Irebu.   No work is done, but all the Chiefs come in to call on the Commandant, who is evidently regarded as a species of parent. Indeed, the nickname of Commandant Jeniaux is the native word meaning Father.   All the sick are brought in and receive treatment; children are vaccinated, and any little native disputes are brought before him to settle.   These nearly always relate to women.   One man will complain that his wife has not behaved herself properly at home, that she has not prepared his food nicely, or much more rarely, that she has run away with another.   Sometimes a Chief complains that another one has stolen some of his women or goats, and then the other side is heard and the judgment pronounced.   These are of course, not formal trials, and the judgment is more in the shape of advice. It is however, always acted upon, for the time being at least.   Serious cases are left to the Courts, but this institution of friendly palavers is an excellent one and establishes confidence and good will among the natives.   It is here indeed, that the personal character of the white man is put to the test.   A calm, just, firm rule will win both the love and respect of these over-grown children, but an excitable, harsh, uncertain temper and manner, will only awaken distrust and hatred.   The more popular the head of the Station, the easier it is for him to find workers in the villages, which in turn affect the general condition of the country around.   Although the system of work is absolutely uniform and every official is tied in a particular groove, yet the whole welfare, work, and indeed, appearance of the country and villages, is good or bad according to the moral character and personality of the chief white man in

NATIVE CHIEFS AT COQUILHATVILLE.

the neighbourhood. I would therefore, say, with however some reserve, that when the natives are discontented and rebel, it is not because they dislike the system of Government, but are dissatisfied with the man who administers it.

On August 16th, Inspecteur d'Etat Warnant, Commander in-chief of the Force Publique, arrives at Irebu. He is on a tour of inspection, and has every reason to be satisfied with the efficiency of the troops. Perfect discipline and harmony is maintained throughout all ranks and all the officers are agreed that the troops are perfectly steady when fighting and never show the least sign of cowardice. Many are very good shots and their drill certainly leaves nothing to be desired.

On the same day Mr. Joseph Clarke, of the American Baptist Mission at Ikoko, calls at Irebu and kindly invites me to his house for a few days. This is situated on the banks of Lake Tumba, or Mantumba or Lac N'Tomba, whichever you prefer. Lors Mountmorres remains at Irebu, but I leave in Mr. Clarke's boat, propelled by twenty four paddlers, and journey along the canal, which twists and turns in all directions. Towards sunset we land at Boboko where Mr. Clarke buys some ducks and eggs, the price of the latter being a table-spoonful of salt for each. He arranges also to sell some nails to the Chief. We then cross the canal to Itutu, a branch Mission Station conducted by a native who preaches, and is an excellent carpenter. Here we sleep, Mr. Clarke making up a bed in the boat, while I occupy a mud hut which however, is scrupulously clean.

Next morning, after a bathe in the canal, in which the

6

water is like warm, weak coffee, we continue our journey
to Ngero, a long straggling village on the north bank of
the Lake.   The huts here are oblong and strongly constructed of hard cane and mud, the roofs being thatched
with dried palm leaves closely interlaced.   It is necessary
to stoop to enter them, for the doors are not five feet high,
but it is possible to stand upright within.   There is
usually a wood fire burning, but no outlet for the smoke,
which slowly finds its way through the roof.   The rafters
therefore, are covered with a kind of tar which, undoubtedly, acts as an antiseptic, and also keeps away the
insects.   The mosquitoes indeed, will not face wood
smoke, but tobacco smoke is useless as a shield against
their attacks.   Both sexes here are practically nude.   The
men are fishermen and the women look after the banana-
plantations, crush the palm nuts for oil and do the cooking and housework.

Ngero was the village of the Chief Lokolo Longania,
who raised a rebellion against the State some years ago,
and after some trouble was captured and hanged.   Here
we buy some fish and eggs and then go on to Ikoko, the
crew singing native songs and Christian hymns as they
paddle along.   The Mission house is very prettily situated,
and is a wooden building, with that very rare luxury in
the Congo, glass windows.   Here we are met by
Mrs. Clarke, who has spent many years with her husband
in Africa.   The Mission has a good farm and garden, and
since the climate is not as bad as in many parts,
its inmates enjoy fair health.   A large wooden building
is used as a chapel and school, and near it is a saw pit
and a carpenter's shop where the boys make furniture and

boxes for sale at Irebu and other Posts in the neighbourhood, for the furniture of the Ikoko Mission is quite
famous.   The girls all wear plain, blue frocks which they
make themselves, as well as clothes for sale, and many
are also quite expert at various kinds of fancy needle-
work.   The business has however, decreased lately owing
to the decrease in population.   The Mission bell has been
ingeniously fixed in a tree, and it calls to school, to work
and prayer, as regularly as the bugle in the State Posts.

The village of Ikoko consists of groups of huts separated from each other by the tall grass, which here is eighteen or twenty feet long, but as the ends bend over, not
above twelve or fifteen feet high.   The people seem idle,
contented and happy, the chief industry being fishing and
net-making.   Mr. Clarke said the population used to be
about 2000 in number, but many have died of Sleeping
Sickness and some have migrated.   This is very evident,
for a number of huts are deserted, and the weeds have
grown over them, in some cases entirely blocking the
entrances.   Out of curiosity, we have a rough census taken
and find there are 138 men in the village on August 19th.
Some no doubt are fishing, and allowing for these and the
women and children, there are probably not more than
1000 to 1200 people now living in the village.   The work
these do for the State, consists of supplying 600 rations of
fish per week to the plantation of Bikoro, a ration consisting of a whole, a half, or a quarter of a fish according to its
size.   For this they are paid 600 mitakos—or about 25/—.
They also supply bamboos and baskets, but it is very plain
that if the people worked hard, they would certainly
not require as long as 40 hours a month to accomplish

their tasks. The fish are caught in nets made of thin bamboo lashed together by a tough creeper, which are arranged in the lake. Sometimes it happens that the fishermen are unfortunate and then they buy from their neighbours who take advantage of the scarcity value and charge them more than they will receive from the State. A village might thus be out of pocket by the transaction, but as each one has its turn, probably by the end of the year no one has lost or gained.

In the Mission school men, women, and children are learning to read and write the native language, and some have mastered also the rudiments of arithmetic and French. Some of the classes are held in the school-room and others under trees near at hand. An assistant missionary, Mr. Whitman, helps Mr. Clarke, while Mrs. Whitman teaches in the school.

On August 20th we start for Bikoro under a threatening sky. It is indeed soon apparent that a tornado is crossing the Lake towards us, for great banks of dense clouds advancing rapidly from the south west now obscure the sun. It would be impossible to travel through the storm, so we turn the boat and make for a creek which bounds Ikoko on the east. Only just in time, we reach a native hut, as a terrific storm bursts over-head. The rain descends in sheets accompanied by vivid green lightning and crashes of thunder. Fortunately the roof is water-tight, but the mud floor of the hut has worn down below the level of the ground outside and soon the water pours through the door and is nine or ten inches deep inside. The fire splutters out and the logs float around amid the crowing of fowls and the cackling of ducks who are quite

contented and happy. Our hostess with a baby strapped
on her back in the usual native fashion, commences to
bale out the water with a basket while we sit on logs in the
darkness and try to keep dry. After about an hour the
storm passes and we go back to the Mission, the Lake
now appearing like a small sea.

Mr. Clarke lends me a copy of the *Memorial concerning
conditions in the Independent State of the Congo* which
was presented to the American Senate early in 1904.
There seem to be a great many curious errors in it. It
starts with the astounding statement that the Congo Free
State has a sea board of 400 miles along the Atlantic,
whereas a glance at the map will show that it is really
about a tenth as long. It estimates the Force Publique
at 30,000 men, rather more than twice its full strength,
and its author is under the impression that the people may
not collect the produce of the land or « barter it for merchandise. » It is a little difficult to understand what the
author means here. As a matter of fact, the people are
trading with each other, all day long and with the white
travellers whenever they have the opportunity. They sell
food, lances, native knives and all kinds of curiosities to
those who desire them and are at perfect liberty to barter
away all their property if they wish to do so. They may
not of course enter the territories of the State or Private
Companies and take the ivory or rubber, any more than
the people in Europe may walk on to private land and
gather the corn or fruit from it for their own use or profit.
The native indeed is in the position of a farm labourer who
gathers the fruits of the soil for his master and is paid a
wage for so doing. On Sunday I attend service in the

chapel. A native from Sierra Leone reads a lesson from the Gospel of St. Matthew, which has been translated into Bangala and gives a short address on the subject afterwards. He is evidently much in earnest and talks with that kind of spirit of conviction frequently to be noticed in street preachers. Several hymns are sung and then the people pass out, dropping their mitakos into the plate as they do so. In the afternoon, we walk round the village. Mr. Clarke notices a boy with a malformation of one knee and speaks to him. He then explains to me that this is another atrocity, for the boy said he had been shot by the soldiers of the State when an infant. An examination of the boy however, showed he was suffering from a kind of bony tumour. There are several chiefs in Ikoko and one of them also practises as a doctor. He has cleared a space about ten feet in diameter and enclosed it for a consulting room, while an inner chamber, still more closely surrounded, is the secret place where the infusions are made and the charms and fetishes consulted. Although many of the drugs used, are efficacious or not, according to the faith of the patient, as in civilised countries, yet the white people constantly tell of apparently wonderful cures by native doctors, and it is certain that the people at present prefer to be treated by those of their own colour. There is also an old lady in Ikoko, the widow of a chief, who is reported to be very clever as a healer. This old person has European features but has an unpleasant expression. The native women wear nothing but a thin belt with a small piece of cloth attached but they are covered with brass rings, and the principle wife of an important chief here was wearing a necklet of solid brass which must

THE FARM AT EALA.

have weighed thirty or forty pounds. This was fixed on and had to be worn night and day.

In spite however, of clever doctors, the men do not live to be much over forty years of age. Perhaps they have too many wives for there are far more old women than men. On the other hand, as there must be two or three women to each man, it is only natural to find more of the former at any given age. The infants are not weaned for three or four years and during that period the woman it is said refuses to lie with her husband. Another wife therefore, cohabits with the man while the first rears her child. Polygamy is thus a custom which the missionaries find very difficult to change. The State however, refuses to recognise more than one wife and many of the soldiers are legitimately married by the officials qualified to perform that office.

Much palm wine is consumed by the natives for its manufacture is very simple. A gourd is tied to an upper branch of a palm which is then tapped and the sap drops into the vessel. If this is left all night, fermentation takes place without artificial aid, and at midday a kind of highly scented alcoholic cider is produced which however, is acid and undrinkable by the evening. This natural wine must therefore, be drunk on the day of fermentation and does not improve on keeping

What a useful tree the palm is! Its trunk, branches and leaves are fine building materials; its matting forms beds and furniture; its oil gives light, acts as butter or lard for cooking, makes soap when mixed with banana juice or an alkali, and indeed, can be used for all the purposes of oil; it forms wine, and the heart of the plant is most excellent eating as a salad.   Therefore given meat, the palm tree and the banana, and a town can be built and its inhabitants fed.   Both sexes smoke a great deal of tobacco and also Indian hemp, which latter has however, been found so injurious that it is illegal to grow the plant but the native tobacco is not at all unpleasant when smoked in a pipe.

On August 22nd we take a trip up a small river to the East of Ikoko which winds through dense forest and is evidently full of fish, for at intervals, barricades are erected which stretch right across the river, with the exception of a small space to allow canoes to go up and down.   In the middle or one side however, an opening is left which can be closed by lowering one of the bamboo nets heavily weighted, vertically down.   Platforms are erected ten or twelve feet high to raise or lower these nets and the whole structure is ingeniously and strongly put together.   The fish are thus allowed to swim up and are then enclosed in a section of the river, when they are easily caught in baskets.   All the riverside population engages in fishing.   On the way I shot a toucan, which must have weighed ten or twelve pounds, with number five shot which happened to be in the gun at the time.   The bird however, was hit in the head and breast. The natives at once plucked it and having scarcely warmed it at the fire greedily eat it.

At a village called Bokoto a boy was brought to me with his right hand missing, for I was very anxious to see an original of the photos which are so common in England. I was indeed beginning to despair of finding one at all for most of the white men had never seen a case, none of the

natives understood what I wished and hitherto no missionary knew where one was to be found.   Here however, was a boy with his right hand missing and it had
evidently been removed by a sharp instrument, but not
I think by a surgeon, for the scars were not such as follow
amputation at the wrist joint.   Mr. Clarke acted as interpreter and the following conversation took place.
    — When was this done?
    — During the rubber war when the boy was an infant.
    — Who did it?
    — The soldiers who came from Bofiji.
    — Why did they come?
    — Because the natives had not collected rubber.
    — Where did this take place?
    — In the country behind Bikoro and the mother was
killed at the same time as she was carrying away her infant.
    Neither the date nor the age of the boy is known, but
he appears to be 12 or 13 years of age and his name is
Imputela.   Although therefore, no proof can be adduced,
for the child of course remembers nothing and only knows
what he has been told, there is a possibility that a native
soldier may have cut off his hand.   On the other hand, it
may have been injured or cut by a native chief.   I mention this case at length, because it was the only one I ever
found in a tour of several thousand miles in the interior of
the Congo State, although everyone knew I was very
anxious to see such cases.   On our way back we call at
Inkaka another fishing village.   Behind it a few of the
Batoir tribe had temporarily settled.   They are very savage
and uncivilised and lead a wandering life, hunting game.
Sometimes they act as professional hunters and are

employed by villagers to find them food. One young fellow was armed with a bow and wooden arrows poisoned at the tip and carefully wrapped in a leaf. The poison is simply the decomposing matter of dead men or animals. As long as this is wet, it is most deadly but loses its strength when dried. For this reason only is the tip wrapped in a leaf. Death has followed within a few hours of being struck with a poisoned arrow and this is only to be expected, for we know how dangerous it is for surgeons when they wound themselves during an examination of the dead body. On the way home we found a snake in the water and shot it just at the very moment it had seized a fish and was holding it in its mouth. Just as we were picking this out another similar one appeared and this met the same fate. They were bright green in colour and had small heads, but one measured 93 and the other 90 inches in length.

On August 23rd we visit Bikoro a large State plantation of coffee, cocoa and rubber, situated on the bank of the Lake about eight or nine miles from Ikoko. It is conducted by Mr. Monaie, a Swiss gentleman, who has had much experience in horticulture. Here nature has been closely imitated but improved upon. First the undergrowth was cleared from the forest and then the native rubber vines were planted and have commenced to climb the trees. These are not tapped until they are ten years old, for although it is possible to obtain the rubber milk before, the vines are killed or seriously injured if they are cut when too young. Some rubber shrubs from Brazil have also been planted, but do not flourish as well as the native kind. Altogether more than a 1000 hectares have been planted and the various plantations are connected by well kept paths. More than three hundred natives are employed and the work in the shade of the forest must be very pleasant. They are housed in a series of huts in a clearing, which are kept scrupulously clean. There are fifteen or twenty soldiers here who act as policemen – for only the big towns have a separate Police force — and guard the rubber and ivory stores. Gum copal is also found in the district in large quantities and in various qualities and colours. The brick houses for the two officials face the lake and gardens have been laid out which are very neat and tidy, the whole place, although much smaller, rivalling even Irebu in beauty.

Next day I return to Irebu in the *Florida* a small stern wheel steamer, and find a welcome mail from home and also a permit to shoot game from Boma. This latter is an imposing document of nine articles and gives permission to shoot adult male animals but not female if accompanied by their young, or, if possible to distinguish them, even if alone. The animals named are, *hippopotames, buffles, antilopes, gazelles, ibex, chevrotains, les divers sangliers, petits singes, outardes, francolains, perdreaux, pintades* and other game birds. Permission it also given to kill « in a scientific manner » one elephant in the close season. It will thus be seen that the State is determined to protect the wild animals of the forest from indiscriminate slaughter and stringent laws regulating hunting are decreed from time to time.

CHAPTER V.

The Ubangi River.—Irebu to Banzyville.

We leave Irebu on August 29th in the *Florida* and
steam up the river Ubangi. The colour of the water at
once changes for whereas the Congo carries much sand
and is brown, the Ubangi carries much clay and is a dirty
yellow. The banks are densely wooded and in the stream
are many islands also covered with forest. Lying on
patches of sand or on the fallen trunks of trees are many
crocodiles asleep. There is not much sport in shooting
them but one which was leisurely swimming up stream
about fifty yards from the ship, made a sporting shot and

was killed with a bullet in the heart. As the cabin is small and hot, we arrange to sleep on the bridge of the steamer which is almost embedded in trees when we tie up to the bank for the night. A tornado bursts about midnight, but the dense foliage acts as a protection and very little water finds its way into our improvised bed-room.

Next day we stop at Bobanghe, a native Wood-Post, and go ashore. The huts here are thatched with grass, for palms seem scarce. Some of the men have black beards which they plait into one or two tails, producing a curious appearance and while they fish, the women do the work of the village and the marketing. Several of them were sitting on logs, contentedly puffing tobacco smoke from wooden pipes while they offered fish, fruit and vegetables for sale to our crew and native passengers. One variety of fish was particulary noticeable; it was coloured like a trout, but had a long snout on the dorsal side. We bought one, and it proved very good eating. The forest here is full of rubber plants, nearly every vine and leaf, when broken, yielding the milky sap which dries, or can be coagulated, into rubber.

One day the boy Jean fell overboard, but leisurely undressed in the water and swam to the bank, whence he was rescued by the canoe of the steamer. He was perfectly calm but Chikaia burst into tears and loudly blubbered. Very little indeed is sufficient to arouse emotionalism in some of the natives, who are always laughing or crying, fortunately the former more often than the latter.

The banks of the Ubangi descend as a rule, sheer into deep water and are often indeed miniature cliffs. No

attempt is made to fashion steps and the villagers slide
down the banks as best they can and thus form a rude
path to the water. A half dozen men in an hour could
make a convenient inclined plain or steps, but the native
only does what work is absolutely necessary in order to
live, and although loving ease, will not take the trouble to
make himself more comfortable. So he climbs painfully
up the bank every night from his canoe and slides down
again every morning without attempting to improve the
path. The vanity of the native however, causes him to
take great pains to—as he thinks—improve his personal
appearance. Brass collars and bangles are very uncommon
on the Ubangi and beads take their place. The women
wear short skirts made of vegetable fibres plaited, which
must take days or weeks to construct. These are black or
red in colour and are suspended from the waist, but as the
fibre is somewhat stiff, they project all round like the dress
of a ballet dancer. These are peculiar to the Ubangi and
are rarely worn by other tribes. The men wear only loin
cloths and often carry a large straight knife suspended by
a leather belt strapped round the chest.

It is very hot from midday to sunset, but the nights
are comparatively cool. One afternoon we saw a great
number of serpent-birds perched high up on a bulbous
tree, and, as they are good to eat, stopped to shoot some.
They were not at all shy and did not depart after several
shots had been fired, but wheeled round and round as if
to discover what was the cause of the strange noise.
Ball, 3 and $5\frac{1}{2}$ shot were equally efficacious and more
than a dozen fell in a few minutes. These birds have a
beautiful black and white plumage with a long neck and

bill and webbed feet and weigh five or six pounds each.
The flavour is somewhat like ptarmigan and the natives
eat them, as usual, without waiting until they were properly cooked.

In the evening I took a stroll in the forest and soon
found the recent spoor of an elephant. Chikaia was just
ahead, when he suddenly stopped and whispered *macat*
pointing in the air. There was a fine monkey and the
boy's instinct for such a choice morsel, actually caused
him to stop, although he knew very well it would have
been absurd to fire and so frighten the elephant. At one
time we must have been within a few yards of the beast
when a snapping of a twig or some sound disturbed him
and with a bellow he rushed away crashing through the
forest. It is curious that while birds are so bold in
Africa, ground game is extremely shy and most difficult to
stalk.

On September 2nd we reach Imese, the first place on
the Ubangi where there are white men. Mr. Donneaux
was the Chef du poste and everything was in good order.
Rubber vines were being planted in the forest and rubber
shrubs in the clearings. Coffee was also growing and
pineapples and other fruits looked well. All the houses
are, as usual, of brick which are of better quality than on
the Congo, as the clay is good and very abundant. The
native village is about ten minutes' walk distant and is
arranged in two or three regular streets and not in patches
of huts dotted down here and there as in the Lake Tumba
District. The State impost here is one kilogramme of
rubber each month from each man for which he is paid
40 or 50 centimes. Collecting this amount takes one or

Young Coffee Trees at Coquilhatville.

two days and the rest of the time the native works for himself or not as he chooses. Here the people seem more industrious than in most parts, many women being engaged in making mats and pottery. The pots are fashioned by hand with the aid of a round stone and are so wonderfully symmetrical that they resemble those made on a lathe. The clay is obtained from the river bed by diving and after the vessel is made, it is first dried in the sun and then baked in a wood fire. While still hot, it is painted with gum copal which renders it watertight.

At dinner we have a dish called « beefsteak American » formed apparently of very tender, cold meat with green salad and mayonnaise. On asking however, we hear it is the raw flesh of goat cut up small. It is certainly the best way of eating goat's flesh, for any method of cooking seems to extract what little juice it possesses and convert it into a substance resembling old leather. The name is curious, for it is neither beef nor steak, and is probably as rare in America as Irish stew is in Ireland or Welsh rarebit in Wales.

There are some very fine canoes here, very often carved throughout their entire length, a favourite device being a crocodile. Two or three very large « tom-toms » are also in the village. These instruments are carved from a solid piece of a tree six or eight feet long, most of the interior being extracted through a narrow slit-like aperture two or three inches wide and running nearly the length of the tom-tom. The result is a hollow instrument, giving one or two different notes when struck in different parts which can be heard for many miles. In case of war, the whole

7

country side can be quickly aroused, but the « tom-tom »
is also used during peace as a telegraph.

At Imese two soldiers and their future brides came on
board for the purpose of travelling to Libenge to be
married, for only Commissaires of Districts and Missionaries
can legally join two into one. The send off was quite
pretty, the happy couples being pelted with flowers as they
stepped on board, while one friend – perhaps a kind of
best man—threw his cap into the river. The State
encourages regular marriages, especially among the
soldiers. The wife then works in the gardens or plantations, while her husband drills, and returns at midday
and in the evening to cook his food.

Next day we reach Dongo, a village situated on a hill
perhaps 200 feet high. After looking at flat forest for
weeks, this appears a veritable mountain and it seems
quite a stiff climb up the rough path constructed as usual
only by the feet of the people who have used it. Mr. Vannini, an Italian officer, is constructing a Post here with
the aid of some ten or fifteen soldiers. Dongo is a very
large village containing perhaps 3000 people and the huts
are arranged in streets running parellel to each other with
their ends towards the river. The physique of the people
is very good indeed, some of the men being more than
six feet in height. The women mostly wear copper collars,
three inches high and with a second horizontal collar
attached on the outside. The whole is hammered on and
must be intensely uncomfortable. A special pillow, consisting of a piece of wood hollowed out for the head is
necessary, as sleep would otherwise be impossible with
such a contrivance round the neck. A great number of

children run about and seem to be well nourished. Some
have large heads and protruding stomachs, without however, other signs of « rickets. » Many of the men are
painted with yellow stripes, an indication that they have
killed their man in battle, and these donned their fighting
clothes of many colours and with shields and spears posed
to be photographed, dancing around and uttering wild war
whoops. A human skull partly buried in the middle of
a road is evidently a souvenir of the terrible orgy which
followed some recent encounter. Indeed all the people
here are cannibals and those killed or captured in war,
except women and children, are always eaten. When not
fighting, the people fish, collect rubber, grow kwanga and
generally work fairly well and are not troublesome.
Mr. Vannini, however, evidently thinks it safer to erect
a high stockade around his house and the huts of the
soldiers. This is a wise precaution, as only a few months
ago four French traders were killed and eaten on the opposite bank of the river.

After passing several densely populated villages, one of
which extends in a straight line for ten miles, we reach
Libenge, the capital of the Ubangi District. The houses
here have been arranged around a square with one side
open to the river. In one of these we take up our quarters
and then go for a stroll with Captain Bertrand, the Commissaire of the District, and Dr. Rhodain, the medical officer
for Ubangi. The latter states that he has only seen two
cases of sleeping sickness in several years' residence and
that there is no syphilis, small-pox or tuberculosis in the
neighbourhood. The people work well here,—the villagers collecting the usual kilogramme per month, while

the workers in the plantations clear the forest and plant more rubber for future use. The hunting here is very good in the dry season. Now however, it is necessary to wade in water three feet deep in the forest. Spoor of elephant and antelope abound and there are several magnificent eagles and hawks overhead.

The chief difficulty here for Europeans is the water question. Although much of this necessity is on all sides, it is not of good drinking quality and dysentery is therefore common, while bilious fever and hematuria are also known.

One night at Libenge as we were playing bridge, the sentry suddenly fired and the bullet whistled uncomfortably close by the door of our house. The guard turned out very quickly without any fuss and passed at the double. A single sharp order was given and then all was quiet again. Next day we heard that a thief had penetrated to the rubber store when he was seen by the sentry, who fired the alarm, but the man was not captured. All the natives here seem anxious to trade. Ladies sell us their brass bangles for a tea cup full of salt and their dresses for a similar amount. Spears, knives and many other curios are also offered for sale some of which have evidently been hastily made since our arrival.

We leave Libenge on September 9th and continue our journey in the *Florida*, this being her first trip up the river higher than this point for at low water, the rapids above cannot be navigated by steamers at all. Now however, the depth is almost at its maximum, and as the boat only draws two feet, she can pass over the rocks with great ease. In the afternoon we stop at a village and ask for wood, for as there was no regular steamer service, there were no organised Wood Posts. The natives at first brought down a log or two and demanded payment at an exorbitant rate, which the captain refused to give, and it became necessary for our crew to go ashore and cut wood themselves. The Chief seemed willing to deal fairly, but evidently had little authority over his lazy people. Then on again through the tornado, which at this season appears daily with great regularity either in the afternoon or at night time. The scenery is now changing, for we are approaching the limits of the great equatorial forest. Hills, which appear like mountains, after the dead level, can be seen in front covered with grass and a few trees.

On September 10th, we reach Songo a small State Post in charge of a native from Sierra Leone. Here we pitch our tents in a clearing and proceed to re-arrange the baggage, for we shall have now to travel in canoes, the river not being navigable for steamers for some distance. Immediately above Songo indeed is the first of the Ubangi rapids, the water roaring and hissing as it fights its way down and over the rocks. Just before bedtime, Chikaia comes with a long face and evidently much disturbed and asks for a gun or rifle to protect himself, as the *indigènes* are supposed to be very savage here. This of course I refuse, and tell him to go to sleep by the fire and not be foolish. However, I notice that both my rifle and gun are loaded and carefully placed by my bedside. The boys then organise a watch over the baggage, taking it in turn to act as sentry. On the opposite side of the river is Bangi, the second most important place in the French Congo, prettily situated on the side of a hill, and next day we cross in a small canoe. The journey is interesting and exciting. Below the rapids are many small whirlpools, and the capita of the canoe takes advantage of these to help him on his course. Sometimes the water at the upper and sometimes at the lower edge of the whirlpool is flowing in the direction he wishes to take and with wonderful dexterity, he turns the bow of the canoe towards a suitable current. We swing about like a cork and ship a good deal of water but arrive without mishap on the other side. We call on Mr. Jacques, the Vice Go.ernor General of the French Congo, who kindly offers us assistance and a few soldiers to act as sentries and interpreters when we camp on the French side of the river. Most of these are Senegalese and are smart looking fellows. The natives here affect a very elaborate head dress consisting of many coloured beads twisted and plaited into their hair, the amount of time and patience required by the barbers being enormous.

It appears that the four French traders, who were massacred a few weeks ago, had two factories, one close to the river and one further inland. In the latter was a large stock of arms and ammunition. These were hastily abandoned and the natives then seized them and attacked the factory on the river. All four white men were killed and it is feared that two were first tied to trees and tortured. A punitive expedition has been sent against the tribe who are now armed with these modern rifles and the moral of the story is obviously that it is very dangerous to permit traders to import and sell arms at all.

One night I was awakened and saw the boys dancing excitedly about the fire and in front of my tent. Having asked the matter, Chikaia, whose zoological knowledge is very limited, replied *il est la petite bête.* This sounded like mosquitoes so, having tucked in my net more closely, I turned round to sleep. A few minutes afterwards, Lord Mountmorres appeared shouting with pain and mounting a chair in front of my tent rapidly peeled off his clothes. He said his bed was full of great black ants which had fixed on his skin and were biting him all over. Millions of these pests indeed were on the camping ground but had as yet not reached my tent. Hastily pulling on high boots and covering myself from head to foot, I cautiously crept out of the tent and found the ground black with ants. It was impossible to kill them by stamping about for they were simply driven into the soft sand and wriggled out again the moment the foot was withdrawn. We were evidently in the line of march of a migrating host and were forced to beat a hasty retreat leaving the insects in full possession.

There is no drinking water at Songo, so we had to boil and filter that from the river. This proved very difficult, for even after allowing it to settle and then carefully decanting it, there was so much mud left, that the pores of the porcelain candles in the filters frequently became blocked. We had therefore to be content with muddy water well boiled. As we had a fair amount of baggage, we required sixty or seventy paddlers and it was not easy to find so many. At length however, after searching on both sides of the river, crews were collected for three large canoes and we arranged to continue our journey on September 14th.

The canoes were lifted up the Songo rapids empty, while the baggage was carried along the bank. It was then stowed in the boats and having taken our places we made a start. The method of propulsion is very interesting to watch. The canoes are sixty or seventy feet long and three or four wide. In the centre is an awning to shade the white man and in front by the bows, a space is left about ten feet long in which three pole men work. These use their poles as in punting, except that the ends are forked, so that they are enabled to push either against the bottom of the river or rocks, or branches of trees on the bank, for the canoe keeps close to the shore all the time in order to give the polemen an opportunity and also to avoid the swifter current running in the centre of the river. In the stern twenty or thirty paddlers sit on the sides of the boat and work together, while on the extreme end two or three stand up with long paddles to steer. The cook with his fire built on a heap of clay in the bottom of the canoe, sits among the paddlers and the sentries and baggage tuck themselves in somewhere, for it is wonderful how many people and how much baggage these canoes will carry.

Soon after starting we pass the Catholic Mission on the French bank and immediately begin to fight a rapid. The paddlers strain every muscle, the pole men push with all their strength against rocks and tree trunks and the soldiers help by pulling on branches of trees or anything else which is fixed. The water whirls past as we creep up inch by inch. At one moment gaining, at another losing, the excitement being intense, for if once we are conquered by the stream, the canoe will probably be broken to pieces on the rocks. At times some of the crew jump out and clinging with their feet to the rocks, while up to their middle in the torrent, push the boat up with all their strength. At length smooth water is reached and on we go quietly for an hour or two, when another rapid is reached and the struggle commences again. The work is intensely hard and dangerous, but the Sangos are expert boatmen and seem anxious to finish their task as som as possible. In rough water or smooth, the crews race along, singing, shouting and encouraging each other to make one more effort. After an exciting and tiring day we reach a village and having seen the crews rationed, pitch our tents.

On again at 6.30. a. m. in a heavy river mist which however, is soon dispersed as the sun rises. The rapids, which at first had the excitement of novelty, began to pall for it was tiresome not being able to read or sleep without being disturbed by the possibility of a bath in a current running, at the rate of perhaps fifteen miles an hour, between rocks. Towards sunset we reach the site of Bokanda, a village now deserted, for some years ago the Chief with his people migrated across the river to the French side. We decide therefore, to sleep in the new village and proceed to cross, but are still in mid stream when we see the majority of the people running away into the forest behind, the women gathering up their children and household utensils, while the men followed more leisurely. The Chief however, and a few braves appear on the beach with guns and for a moment it looks as though they mean mischief. They evidently however think better of it, for we land unmolested and send interpreters to say we are hunters and only desire a place for our camp and food for our men. The Chief at once advances and gives us chickens and eggs while the soldiers pitch the tents in the square of the village.

On again at daybreak, the journey being still more tiring, for it is impossible to force the canoes heavily laden up some of the cataracts. We have therefore to land three times and while the baggage is carried along the bank, the empty canoes are hauled up with ropes. At length the elephant rapids are safely negotiated and an hour or two afterwards Mokoangai is reached but in three long days' hard work, we have ascended only about thirty miles of the river.

At Mokoangai is a large plantation and farm and well built houses for the one or two white men who live there. Next day I start before daybreak hunting. The country is open and hilly, covered generally with grass eight or ten feet high. Still there are many places where the ground is almost bare and it is an ideal spot for stalking game. After walking a few miles in a mist, we see several antelopes and endeavour to stalk them. While still nearly a hundred yards away, they commence to walk slowly towards cover but it is possible to get a fair side shot and one falls heavily hit in the shoulder. Soon after an elephant suddenly appears about two hundred yards ahead walking along the crest of a hill. Sending the native hunter to pick up the antelope, Chikaia and I follow the elephant's spoor for some hours, but do not come up with it or find other game. We were now high up on the range of hills behind Mokoangai and the view was magnificent. The great river could be seen winding its way between the hills covered with the vivid greens only to be found in damp tropical countries. Otherwise the picture somewhat recalled central Wales with a Wye magnified a hundred times.   Chikaia had walked a long way carrying a heavy rifle, and now showed signs of fatigue so he was encouraged by being allowed to shoot a monkey on the way home.

Next day being Sunday, we rest quietly in the Post and prepare to leave next morning in the « Aia » which is one of the first launches Stanley took to Africa and is therefore, somewhat ancient.   Since she is too small to carry much baggage, she tows a large open iron boat nearly the same size alongside.   In this the camp is stowed and the boys and soldiers take their places sitting on the bales and cases, and we make a start on Monday September 19th for Banzyville.   Fortunately there are no rapids in this stretch of the river and it is at least possible to stand up comfortably in the launch, whereas in the canoes, it was necessary to sit still in a long hammock chair for practically twelve hours each day.

The people and villages now change much in appearance for the huts are shaped like beehives and are made of frameworks of wood covered with grass.   The entrance is only about three feet high and the dome of the roof perhaps four times that height.   In some of them a kind of platform is erected which seems to be an attempt to make a two storey building of the hut.   The women are here either quite nude or wear a small piece of cloth or grass below the waist ; the men however all have a loin cloth.   All the people seem to be of fine physique and the proportion of children is abnormally high.   The first night we stop at a trading post of the Dutch Company on the French side of the river and are hospitably received by the agents there.

Next day we reach the Catholic Mission of Sainte Famille also on French territory. The Fathers have laid out a large plantation and farm; horses, cattle, sheep, goats and poultry all doing well. Indeed modern American ploughs and carts give the farm quite a home-like appearance. Maize, oranges, bananas, pineapples and many vegetables are here in abundance. Sleeping Sickness is not known, which immunity is attributed by the priests to the fact that the natives have plenty of fresh meat and eat little kwanga. Apparently the disease is due to a bacillus. It is however, at least possible that the new diet of the civilised native may be a predisposing factor. The savage is naturally carnivorous and before the advent of the white man, had little to eat but animal flesh. Now his chief article of diet in the western parts of the Congo is kwanga, which consists chiefly of starch, and he has only a little meat and fish. Along the Congo where the native is civilised, there is much sleeping sickness, but along the Ubangi where he is more savage, there is practically none. The Falters give us some spirits distilled from the papye and pineapple which are very good and beer made from maize which is not. They then show us round the grounds and before we leave load us with eggs and fresh vegetables which are very acceptable. At sunset we tie up to the bank and make a camp. It is wonderful how quickly the grass is cut down, the tents erected, fires lighted and dinner cooked, for when the native knows he has to perform a certain definite task, he works hard, so that he can eat his dinner and get to sleep as soon as possible. Chikaia apparently has a fine sense of satire or humour. A table was

broken and when I asked how it was done, Chikaia instead
of answering « it has been done a long time » as an European servant would, went one better and said « it has
always been like that. »   « I suppose it was made so, »
I replied.   « Yes, Sir » was the answer and there was no
more to be said.

The banks of the river are here lined with villages and
each time we stop crowds run to see the steamer, while
the Chief comes on board, shakes hands solemnly and
presents eggs, chicken or a goat.   In return we hand back
a good value in cloth, beads or salt.   Mitakos are not
seen here at all, for beads are used instead.   The natives
always seemed grateful and satisfied with their presents,
which was rarely the case on the Congo where the people
generally grumble even when they receive many times the
value of the article they sell.   We camp at the village of
Dru, where we find it very difficult to pitch tents owing
to the rocky nature of the soil.

On September 22nd we reach the Kuangu river where
is situated the chief post of a French Trading Company.
The buildings are as usual of bricks, the mortar being
made of the shells of river oysters and sand.   Soon after
our arrival, a poor native was brought in whose hand had
been terribly mangled in a circular saw.   We dressed it
as carefully as possible and fixed it on a splint until he
could reach a post with a hospital.   In the night however,
weird chanting was heard and next day we discovered
that his friends had been exorcising the evil spirits—i. e.
the perchloride of mercury in which the hand had been
washed—had torn off all the bandages and sent the boy
away in a canoe to avoid the white medicine man.   The

hand will almost certainly fall off and the further history of the boy will perhaps be interesting. One of the traders, Mr. Constantine, a Swiss, said he had been stationed in the interior and had heard no news since January. We are only able to bring him up to June, three months behind date. This gentleman has had an interesting career. He fought for England in the Matabele war and then settled in the Orange Free State where he was commandeered by Cronje and forced into the trenches at Magersfontein, but to his own great satisfaction was soon taken prisoner by the British and was very well treated. He now lives absolutely alone, without a guard of any sort, some days' journey from the river and feels quite safe, for the natives here look upon a white man as a protection from the Arabs. This Company trades in rubber with the natives, paying in beads at the rate of 40 centimes a kilogramme. It is therefore, unlikely that many natives migrate to the French Congo where they receive no more pay for their work than in the State, and are besides taxed. The country behind the station is flat veldt and only a few small elephants are occasionally found. The usual heavy tornado bursts in the afternoon nearly filling the launch and boat with water in a very short time. Having bought some wine and other stores, from the Company we next day continue up the river past many villages all densely populated. The architecture has again changed, the huts now being tent shaped and rising to a point in the centre which is sometimes ornamented with a pair of antelope horns. Some of the villages have plantations and all the inhabitants seem desirous to trade, salt being the substance usually demanded in return for lances, knives or curios. Indeed, even our own people wish to do a little business, and after buying articles from the villagers, try to sell them to us at no doubt a greatly enhanced price. The higher one travels up the river, the more numerous and densely populated are the villages until they extend almost without a break for many miles along the banks. Each one supplies us with a *bras* of wood which is paid for with beads. The scenery here in the very centre of Africa is beautiful, range after range of hills, not however very high, extending as far as the eye can see. These are covered with grass, which near the villages is often burnt off, leaving black patches. On these the manioc will be planted for two years and then new areas will be cleared in the same manner. It is very hot in the day time and very humid, so that it is extremely difficult to preserve anything. Stitches rot in leather and the soles of boots fall off, guns and rifles have to be oiled carefully every day and cigars are completely spoilt in a few hours unless kept in tin boxes. Can one wonder therefore that the human system soon breaks down in this vapour bath and that sickness is very common in this part. There is not much game to be seen from the river but occasionally a covey of partridges rises from the grass and comes within gun shot of the launch.

The day before we reached Banzyville we found the steamer of the French Company and paid a visit to the Director, where we drank to the Anglo-French agreement, news of which had just arrived. Every Frenchman in Africa is delighted with the gift of territory as every Englishman should be with the settlement of so many prickly questions.

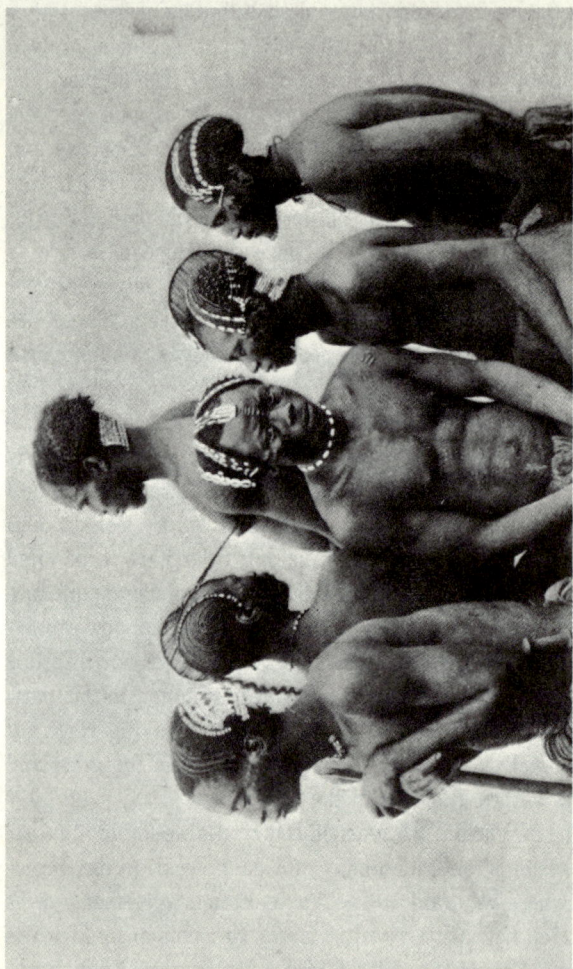

Sango Natives of the Ubangi.

CHAPTER VI.

The Upper Ubangi. — Banzyville to Yakoma.

Banzyville has been built on a beautiful site at a double bend of the river.   Opposite is the French Post of Mobaie and between them roars a rapid.   The country on each side is hilly, while the soil is rocky, great boulders of granite and quartz lying about in isolated grandeur.   We reach the Post on the morning of September 26th and are met by Captain Auita, an Italian, who is the Zone Chief here.   The buildings are arranged on two sides of a square, the other two being formed by the river as it turns to the left, and the open space is covered with gravel

8

which makes a welcome change from sand and clay while
the house placed at our disposal looks particularly inviting after a week of tents and the small launch.   Everything is wet through and has to be spread out on the gravel to dry under nature's great fire.   Unfortunately some
of the skins, which perforce have been left in cases for a
week, under water one minute and baked in the sun the
next, have hopelessly rotted and have to be thrown away.
Next morning we interviewed numbers of native Chiefs
who were all very anxious to exchange lances and other
curiosities for European clothes.   All were content with
« Bulamatadi, » although some grumbled at the necessity
to find porters and paddlers.

    This is evidently one of the most populous districts in
the whole Congo, for on all sides, both at the river edge
and on the hill tops, are large villages consisting of tent-
shaped huts and « shimbeks, ». or square open sheds,
under which the natives sit and sleep most of the day.
Besides rubber, great quantities of rice are grown here,
the plantations extending parallel to the river for more than
two miles.   Here men, women, and children are at work
and those near the road come forward, give a military
salute and shake hands, a custom peculiar to this part,
for hitherto the women have not saluted and only the chiefs
offered the hand.   Many of the people have thin lips and
semitic noses and most are well made.   As usual, if one
meets a husband and wife, the former strolls ahead with
a spear or stick, while the latter follows carrying a baby
riding on one of her hips, tied on by her wrap of cloth, and
with a heavy load of wood or food-stuff on her head.
We cross the river in the evening and dine with Captain

Meilleur at Mobaie.   The French villages are identical
with those on the State side, but the natives are, if possible, still more idle.

Next morning much rubber is brought into Banzyville.
Strings of natives, each with a little basket-full of this
substance, march into the square and sit down in lines on
the gravel.   The baskets are then weighed on a yard arm
and the weights entered in a book by Captain Auita until
a record of the whole has been made when the chattering
throng departs to a shed near by where five cooks have
been hard at work preparing dinner for them.   The natives
here are paid in cloth at the rate of 50 or 60 centimes
a kilogramme according to the quality of the rubber and
although each man is supposed to supply only one kilogramme a month some of the villages here send in more
than a ton in that time.

Mr. Fernaka, the second in command, arrived on the
28th after marching for thirty days in the interior over
unexplored ground.   He said it was mostly marsh land
containing a few villages from which the inhabitants, seeing
the white man approach with his soldiers, fled into the bush.
At first indeed the natives are always fearful of the whites,
but in a short time are willing to trade and soon become
very friendly.   The native, in fact, quickly acquires absolute confidence in Europeans and his fear at first is,
obviously, only the fear of the unknown.   It is rather
amusing to see the children in villages where few white
men have penetrated, run shrieking with terror to their
mothers when a strange looking person, with a white face
and clothes appears.   At the sound of the launch whistle
also many children run away.   One of the soldiers,

a sergeant of some years' standing who accompanied Mr. Fernaka on his arduous march, unfortunately contracted dysentery and arrived at Banzyville only to die. We attend the funeral, the absolute simplicity of the ceremony being very impressive. All the troops here, perhaps seventy or eighty marched with reversed arms to the cemetery after the buglers sounding the Last Post and lined up opposite the grave. The order was given to present arms, the coffin was lowered, each person present threw a handful of earth into the grave and all was over. Far into the night, however, one could hear the mournful dirge the soldiers were chanting for their dead comrade. Hunting here is difficult although game abounds, the grass being high enough to conceal antelopes and everything else except elephants. After a walk through rough country and water for six hours without success, I was glad to get into my hammock and was jogged back home by perspiring natives, who took turns to carry their burden and changed about every ten minutes. Altogether the hammock is not comfortable, and it is obviously useless hunting here until the grass is burnt. Next day, being very tired and stiff, I pass the time looking through *Civilisation in Congoland* again. Having now visited many of the places mentioned in that book, the difficulties which beset a writer who publishes a work on a country he has never seen, become very apparent. In fact, it gives no more idea of the condition of the Congo than a file of the Police News would convey an impression of English civilisation. When one has visited some hundreds of villages and seen perhaps a million of natives, most of whom seem cheerful and contented, one marvels indeed

how such absolutely false reports of the condition of the
country can have originated. On the other hand, it is
impossible to travel several thousands of miles in the Congo
—especially in the unfrequented parts — without constantly
wondering what is the extraordinary power which enables
a few hundred white men, not only to govern as many
million blacks, but to open up and develop a country as
large as the continent of Europe, which a few years ago
was absolutely unknown.

We can dismiss at once the idea that the native is suppressed by military despotism, for the Posts are isolated
and the number of troops in them merely sufficient to guard
property and stores, that is to say, to fulfil the duties of
policemen in England. At any moment the thousands of
natives who live in or near the Posts, could overwhelm
these small forces long before help could arrive from the
next Government Station, in many cases a week's journey
distant. The fact that they do not do so, is at least nega-
tive evidence that the white men do not ill treat the people.
There is however, much positive evidence that the native
has, not only a great respect, but also an affection for his
new rulers, and it is not difficult to understand the reason,
when we compare his fate before the advent of the Europeans with his condition at present.

In each village was a Chief or Chiefs, freemen and slaves
who passed their lives hunting and fighting other tribes.
The sole property of the Chiefs and freemen were their
huts, canoes, and slaves, and the rude instruments they
used in war and hunting. The unfortunate slaves were
bought and sold, captured in war and were often killed
and eaten. One slave was worth so many goats, lances,

or knives, and one large canoe would buy several women. Legislation rested with the Chiefs and trial by ordeal was common, but always so arranged that the result could be controlled by the judge. This is not the place however, to describe these interesting, if horrible practices.

Now at present the people are rich beyond the wildest dreams of their ancestors for the value of the property of the great Chiefs has greatly increased, since they have dealt with Europeans. Again the Chief of a small village containing 1000 men supplies 1000 kilogrammes of rubber each month to the State for 50 centimes a kilo. To collect this amount takes two or three days; each year therefore the village receives £240 for collecting a substance of no value at all to the natives whose daily routine in the meantime is scarcely affected at all. The natives used ivory chiefly to make war horns, but some of the Chiefs had so much that they constructed fences of fine points round their mud huts little thinking that in the white man's country, those useless tusks would be worth a small mountain of salt. Now they exchange them for clothes, cloth, salt, and other useful commodities. The lucky owner of a canoe, it is true, can no longer buy three or four slaves with it, but he can use it to transport produce or to catch fish, for which he is well paid. Again compare the lot of the slave in the past with his present condition. He was liable to the most terrible fate at any moment; now he can enter the army, work in the plantations or remain safely in his village and do a few hours' work each month. There is however, another force acting which we should hardly expect would affect the mind of a savage. He is greatly influenced by a desire to

Young Sango Girls at Banzyville.

ascend the social ladder at the summit of which, is of course, the white man, and anyone having direct dealings with him, at once knows himself to be superior to the naked cannibal of the forest. The servant, or « boy, » of the white man, holds a high rank and considers himself to be quite another species of man than his cousin, who is still uncivilised. So also the soldiers and workers in the plantations, who come into daily contact with the officials. All the most intelligent and ambitious natives are thus drawn away from their primitive condition of life and become attached to their masters, who give them cloth to wear and beads with which to beautify themselves. The most important Chiefs are as anxious indeed to appear like Europeans, as a prosperous native of Sierra Leone, is to wear patent boots and carry a silk umbrella. There is one near here named Bayer, a young man of much intelligence and business capacity, who has built himself a brick house, dresses like a European, and is a proud man when he is asked to smoke a cigar on the verandah of the mess. The Chiefs are, however, never asked to eat with the Europeans, a distinction which is both necessary and wise.

It daily becomes more and more obvious that the white man is greatly respected and that his word is absolutely trusted. What he says is true and what he promises, he does. The native appears to respect these characteristics perhaps all the more because he is so lamentably deficient in them himself.

It is indeed the respect caused by moral not physical force which enables a few Europeans to govern this great country with success, and permits one or two white men to live securely with a few soldiers in an isolated Post surrounded by thousands of natives most of whom are savage cannibals.

There are, however, many difficulties yet to be surmounted, and among them is the arrangement of a satisfactory currency. This was brought home forcibly on October 1st when according to weekly custom, the people in the villages around brought in food for the Post. Many women appeared with large bunches of bananas for which as a rule, they are paid by beads. In this prosperous part the heads of the women are already fully adorned with beads and most of their household ornaments also, so they demanded cloth instead.

The question of the currency is a very difficult one. There is the danger of flooding the banks of the Congo with mitakos, and the banks of the Ubangi with beads. In other words these articles which function as money are not used as rapidly as they are supplied, and a lady whose limbs are already weighted with brass rings and whose head is heavy with beads, wishes for some other payment. There is a warehouse at each of the State Posts in which cloth, clothes, beads, salt, and many other commodities likely to be of use to the natives are kept, but it is manifestly impossible to give as wages to each individual the particular object he desires at the particular moment. The objection to beads and mitakos, does not apply to salt and cloth, the former being at once consumed, and the latter being worn out in course of time. Nevertheless it is not well to have a currency which is continually being formed only to be destroyed. The money currency, already existing in the Lower Congo will, however, in course of time be extended, but there are still many diffi-

culties in the way.   Francs and centimes will of course be
of no use to the natives, unless Stores are still kept at the
State Posts at which they can buy whatever they wish.
This great question is, however, occupying the careful
attention of the Government, and will no doubt be settled
as satisfactorily as many others have been which were
equally difficult.

Sunday is always an interesting day in a State Post, for
the Chiefs with many followers come in for a friendly chat
and to ask advice.   October 2nd was particularly exciting
for a new Chief had been elected in a village near Banzyville, and great rejoicings consequently followed.   Singing,
shouting, dancing and a general hubbub, went on from
morning to night, and if the desire to make a noise is any
criterion of happiness, these people must be the happiest
in the world.   There are many forms of dances; sometimes each one shuffles his legs without moving more
than a foot or two and then swings his arms, head and
body solemnly backwards and forwards; sometimes a
number will form a ring, and one after the other will leap
into it and rapidly rotate themselves; but whatever the
form, all seemed to be keenly excited and to enjoy it
thoroughly.

The natives near the Ubangi have a very distinctive
tatouage.   It consists of five elevated knobs of skin which
form a straight line continuing the line of the nose up the
forehead.   These are formed by making for each knob two
parallel incisions in the skin about half an inch apart and
lifting the flap between.   A piece of ivory is then inserted
under the flap and left in until the wound has healed, the
result being a knob of skin elevated above the level of the

rest of the surface. All the tatouage in the Congo consists in raising the skin in this manner, but in each district the design is different. Simple tatooing by pricking in colours does not appear to be practised at all.

Fishing here is very simple and very effective. Large baskets tapering to a point and open at the broad end are fixed by ropes, or rather by the strong vines which function as ropes here, just at the top of the rapids and the water rushes through with great force. The fish are carried into the baskets, but cannot pass through or return against the current, and are then simply speared and lifted out. They have firm, white flesh and are good eating.

On October 3rd the Chief of the Banzas comes to the Post to call. He is a fine, intelligent-looking man and rules his people, who are very numerous, admirably. In this part of the Congo, the chieftainship descends from father to son, but in some districts the succession passes through the family of the wife of the Chief.

Numerous petty Chiefs drop in to the Post at intervals during the day and are rather a nuisance, for they are always begging for clothes and offering lances and presents in exchange. They do not realise that one does not carry a superfluity of clothes when travelling, or that one or two lances are quite sufficient to keep as curios. Probably they think we are traders for we are not *bulamatadi*, and no one I believe, has ever ascended the Ubangi on a pleasure tour before. The newly-elected Chief was very anxious to be given a suit of clothes as he had none and wished to make an impression on his new subjects. He described with many gestures, that he was elected with much beating of drums, which indeed was only too true and said he always intended to remain a great friend of the State.   After that, of course he had to be given some clothes.   The system of giving « tips » indiscriminately is however, carried much too far in the State, and if it is not stopped, will soon prove to be a very heavy tax on the white man.   Every native demands a tip on every possible occasion whether he has done a service or not, and if he has done some work and is only paid his due, is as discontented and abusive as a cabman who has only received his legal fare.

There are many native thieves all over the Congo — one of them actually penetrated into the house of Captain Auita at midday in bright sunshine and stole a spear and a native knife.   He was however, soon caught and marched off to prison.   Trials by ordeal used to be very common among the natives.   A favourite method was to give a dose of strychnine to a fowl and if it died, the accused was guilty, but if it lived, he was innocent.   The wretched fowl, feeling in any case very ill, walked about wondering at the excitement and followed by the complainant shouting « die, die, die, fowl » and the defendant shouting « live, live, live, fowl. »   The strength of the solution was always arranged by the judge so the verdict was known to him beforehand.   A curious instrument to take the place of a jury, is a nut through which a piece of fibre has been passed in such a way, that when it is held vertically, the nut slides up and down.   By a curious twist of the fibre however, it is possible to prevent the nut falling.   At the trial, the nut is raised to the top of the string and if it stays there, the accused is innocent, but if it falls, he is guilty. Here again, the judge can make the machine decide either way at his will.

Among the many objectionable insects of the Congo is the « jigger, » a kind of sand fly which burrows under the skin, usually of a toe, and deposits eggs in a sack there. Unless these are removed an abscess forms. The natives sit about calmly removing jiggers from each other's feet with needles, and show considerable skill in this small operation. It is necessary therefore never to move about with bare feet, for the boys carry them into every place.

Much ivory comes into the Post at intervals, the points sometimes weighing 70 or 80 lbs. each. The State preserves the elephant very strictly, and the export duty on tusks above 6 kilos in weight, is 21 frs. per kilo. Still it is not likely that the Congo will continue to yield such large quantities of ivory, for the elephant only bears one offspring in three years and the growth of the baby is very slow. There is a baby elephant here one year old. He stands about 4 feet, 6 inches high, and has no sign of tusks at present. He is fed on rice, milk and bananas and is a playful little fellow. A tame ape here fears the elephant very much and at his approach at once clings to the native who tends him or climbs over his shoulder, so as to place the boy's body always between himself and the elephant.

On Monday October 10th we prepare to continue our journey up river. We shall now require six or seven canoes, as they are not so large as the ones lower down and our crews, servants, escort and camp followers total up to nearly two hundred. Captain Auita sends a few State capitas with us and Captain Meilleur lends us some

French soldiers belonging to the 1st Senegalese Tirail-
leurs, a splendid set of fellows, very smart in their khaki
uniforms.   We can, therefore, land with impunity on
either side of the river, *i. e.* in the French or the State
Congo, and be able to communicate with the Chiefs, for it
will be rather difficult perhaps to feed so many people.

Next day we start amid the most terrific din.   Each of
the seven canoes carries one or two tom-toms and some
have also native bells.   All the capitas and most of the
paddlers shout orders to each other which no one regards,
even if they hear them, while the friends of the paddlers
howl farewells from the beach.   At length however, the
baggage is arranged and the little fleet starts in single file,
for each canoe hugs the bank.   Before half an hour had
elapsed my canoe struck a rock and stuck on it.
Fortunately we were not travelling faster than two miles
an hour, or a hole would have been made in the bottom.
As it was, it was necessary for half the crew to go overboard,
stand on the rock, and lift the canoe off.   Never was
a ship so speedily lightened, and in a few moments
we were once more afloat.

The river now passes through a kind of gorge not more
than half a mile wide and continues between hills clad with
long grass but after an hour or two, it widens out again
and the banks become low.   The heat is great and the
unceasing blows on the tom-tom within three feet of one's
ears are very annoying, but if it is stopped, the crew no
longer keep good time, and the boat, therefore, travels
very slowly.   The singing, on the other hand, is by no
means unpleasant.   One of the crew sings a solo, a kind
of recitative, the words being an extempore criticism, as

a rule, of the white passenger, and then the whole join in chorus in perfect harmony. The music is now wild and weird, now passionate and joyful, but always natural. There is nothing of the catch penny type of ditties, which become popular in England and America, in these savage African songs, nor are they in the least like Chinese or Indian music. The instruments are rudimentary; simple zithers, rattles, bells and a kind of guitar, but it is probable that all these, except the bells, have been introduced by the Europeans or Arabs.

On we creep slowly until we reach the island of Ya which belongs to the State. All the other islands, except Bamu, being no man's land. Here we land at a large village and while the boys are arranging the camp, we see that our party are all fed. The Chiefs are requested to provide food, and soon nearly two hundred women appear, each with a wooden vessel containing a ration of kwanga, palm oil, salad, bananas, plantains, fish, meat, or a general mixture. These they deposit on the ground and stand at attention each behind the meal she has prepared. The sergeants and capitas distribute the rations among the soldiers and paddlers, and at an order of the Chief, the whole crowd disappears into the huts. Then we eat our dinner, consisting of the usual chicken and eggs, have a game of two-handed bridge and turn in.

Suddenly shrieks are heard coming from a hut and we order the sentry to discover the cause. He soon appears with one of our paddlers, who states that another one stole his ration, and when he endeavoured to get it back, beat him severely. We order him therefore more food, and decide to investigate the case in the morning.

Next day after giving cloth to the Chiefs in payment for the food, we send for the youth who made so much noise in the night. A poleman now stated that the boy had stolen his loin cloth and that therefore he had beaten him. This story contradicted the other and further native evidence complicated the story still more, so after explaining to the poleman that he had no right to beat the boy, even if he were one of his crew, and that if such a thing occurred again, he would be severely punished, we decided to take no further action.

One of the French soldiers now appeared and told a romantic story. He had found a long lost blood sister in the village, the mutual recognition being confirmed by the tribal marks. Both had been sold as slaves when children; he had drifted into the French native army and she had married one of the subjects of the State. Now she wished to leave her husband and go away with her brother, who was willing to pay compensation for her loss if necessary. As this seemed to raise some delicate questions, we refused to take any step, except to report the matter to the proper authorities.

After these delays, we started up the river, lined on both sides by thickly populated villages. About midday an excited crowd stopped us at one of these and asked for our help. As everyone shouted at once and probably no one told the truth, it was difficult to discover what was the matter, but some women were missing from the French Congo and an elephant from the State, and the natives on each bank wished the white men to punish those on the other. As private travellers, of course we could take no action, even if we had wished, and continued on our way already two or three hours late. At length at 6 p. m., Zinga is reached, a large village with a fine plantation, and here we camp.

Just above the village the rapids are so strong that it is dangerous to take the canoes up charged, and it is necessary to carry all the baggage for about three miles across country until smooth water is reached again. The capitas wished to attempt the ascent with the canoes full, for the native dislikes carrying, more than anything else. We explain that if it is necessary for the white men, who can swim, to walk, how much more necessary is it to carry the baggage, which would at once sink if the canoes capsized. However, this did not convince them and Europeans who have had accidents on the river say, that although the whole crew, who all swim like fishes, go to the assistance of the white man when a canoe capsizes, not one will take the trouble to rescue the baggage. Probably the native, whose personal property is limited to a loin cloth, thinks all other possessions are useless vanities and not worth troubling about. The view here is very beautiful, the river taking a double bend between hills which are well wooded and traversed by mountain torrents of clear water hastening to join the main stream roaring in its rocky bed below. Numerous pintades are usually found here, the finest game bird for eating in the whole of Africa, and I go ahead of the bearers to search for them, but see nothing of interest.

By 8 a. m. the canoes have all passed the rapids, and are charged again, so once more we make a start. Soon another rapid is reached which it is impossible to negotiate with the paddles. Some of the crew therefore, go overboard and standing on the rocks up to their waists in water, literally lift the boat up foot by foot until the top is

The State Post at Djabir.

reached.   After this the river widens again and the current
is not so strong.   One of the canoes is now reserved as
a kitchen and carries the goats, chickens and other food.
It is interesting to watch Luembo silting smoking his pipe
over the fire as he cooks the lunch.   Nothing disturbs his
calm serenity and he goes on philosophically making soup
even in the roughest water.   When lunch is ready we stop
by the bank, the kitchen comes alongside and the hot,
strong soup is very acceptable, for it is impossible to eat
much in the heat of the day.

At night time we decide to stop at the mouth of the Koto
river, where is a post of the Trading Company of that
name, and the two agents there kindly extend hospitality to us.   Some of the natives here show well marked
semitic features and a few, oddly enough, have eyes
shaped like the Chinese.   They are all ready to bring
rations for the paddlers and accept payment without
comment.   Indeed, the native never says « thank you, »
but as he speedily lets you know when he is dissatisfied,
silence obviously means contentment.   The Company has
a rubber plantation and a well kept farm with cows, pigs
and sheep which live healthily here.

The Koto river is almost as large as the continuation
of the Ubangi and rises far away up north.   Passing it
we continue ascending between banks, on which villages
are practically continuous the whole way until we reach
Gumba, a large village on the French side with a hospi-
table Chief and a mud guest house.   In this we store the
baggage and arrange to sleep on the verandah which has
fortunately a watertight, roof for the almost daily tornado
happened to be of an unusually violent description.   The

9

lightning is practically continuous and of a vivid, blinding green colour; the thunder sounds as if whole streets have been struck and knocked down, while the rain descends like the stream of a shower bath.

The Chief's house in this village is oblong, but at the two ends of the roof, spire-like tops are affixed, similar to those on the rest of the huts in the village. They are not ornamental nor useful, but interesting as marking a native characteristic on a house copied from those in the Government Posts.

Next morning it was still raining hard, so we waited in the dry without anxiety, as we knew the journey to Yakoma would only take five or six hours, but about 10 a. m. having emptied the canoes, which were full of water, we arranged the baggage and made a start. Village succeeded village, in which were numerous people elaborately decorated with beads and paint, but not otherwise covered. All the Chiefs were well disposed and presented eggs or chicken, and took the cloth or salt offered in return without grumbling. About midday we reached the commencement of the Yakoma village, which extends for some miles along the bank. Most of the crew were evidently well known here and several lived in the village. Their well-meaning friends therefore, jumped on to the canoes as they passed or swam out to them and took the paddles and poles from their tired comrades. With a greatly augmented company, with the canoes dangerously deep in the water, with tom-toms beating, bells ringing, bugles sounding and people shouting, we arrived at Yakoma about 5 p. m. on October 15th thus completing a voyage along the whole length of the Ubangi river.

CHAPTER VII.

Yakoma to Djabir.

Yakoma is built on the banks of the Uele just before it joins with the Bomu to form the Ubangi. The voyage up that river from its entrance into the Congo to its source here occupied seven weeks of which half the time, however, was spent in State Posts. Canoe travelling is terribly tiring, although one merely sits still in a hammock chair all day, and it has not been by any means comfortable camping in the forest during or after the daily tornado. Still the trip has been very interesting for this is one of the least known parts of the world and the people are probably the least civilised.

This experience brought home the fact with something like a shock that human nature is much the same everywhere and that if the savage leads the life practically of an animal, he is at the same time not very much unlike modern civilised man. He does not wear clothes, but he is very vain and adorns himself with beads and bangles, his hair dressing requiring hours of patient labour. He is often as pleased at being photographed as a young fashionable beauty and, if a warrior, is as proud of the paint which shows he has killed some one in battle, as a soldier is of his medals. He is frankly commercial in his dealings and as anxious to say what he thinks will please his guest as the most tactful of society's hostesses. He is as keen to win in a canoe race as any undergrad in his college boat and is a genuine and true sportsman. He is very jealous as a husband and devoted as a father, characteristics common both to animals and to the most intellectual of men. He is, as a Chief, by no means hard on his subjects although his punishments are barbarous and his sense of justice not greatly developed. He eats human flesh but not the diseased livers of geese and he prefers his meat decomposing as some like their game. He takes no more thought for the morrow than many civilised people who live from hand to mouth without considering the future and finally he sees the world from his point of view and has little desire to discuss that of others. Mr. Van Luttens the Chef du Poste kindly meets us and places a house at our disposal. We then read our mail, the first news from home since July, and glance through the newspapers. The country around Yakoma is flat and as there is no sign of forest, the plantation consists of rubber bushes only. Much rice is also grown here and at one time a large amount of coffee was raised from plants brought from Liberia but these have since died. The native coffee, however, does well and is certainly as good as any in the world, so it seems to be wiser to cultivate this and to leave foreign varieties alone.

This is one of the very few places in the Congo where

the cows give more milk than is required by their calves, and where butter can be made. The farm is well stocked with horses and cattle for breeding purposes which function they fulfil very well, the foals and calves looking strong and healthy. All the Chiefs in the neighbourhood come and call upon us. They are all very rich, powerful and loyal in this district and delight in wearing European clothes or uniforms. One of them was dressed in an old naval uniform with an antique sword and another as a captain in the State service although he had no right to wear the uniform of the Force Publique at all. Just opposite Yakoma on the opposite bank of the Uele is a village for retired soldiers where they have their own gardens and plantations and live a life of ease but are not pensioned. The term of service is for three or seven years with option of signing for another three years after the long period with increased pay and another three years if desired after that. It is not at all uncommon to find sergeants who have served ten or twelve years and they are always very responsible men.

As usual the people offer us many native articles in return for cloth and we add to our already large collection.

As there is no big game near at hand I decide to make a collection of small birds, of which there are very many here, with most beautiful plumage. Unfortunately I have no smaller shot than $5\frac{1}{2}$ and it is difficult to avoid damaging the smaller varieties. However, by firing with the full choke barrel at about fifty yards two or three pellets almost always hit even the smallest birds. A very good method of preserving them is to inject formol into the bodies which at once stiffen out and become rigid in any position they are placed. Birds can thus be set with the wings extended in a flying position or as if roosting the effect being much prettier than any which can be obtained by stuffing. If is however, necessary to arrange them and inject very soon after they are dead for if rigor mortis once sets in, it is impossible to alter the position assumed by the head and wings. There were great numbers of beautiful birds in the plantation and it was easy to obtain over a dozen different specimens in less than an hour (1). Redlegged partridges are also found here in the rice, but as in Europe this variety will not rise and one may walk all day hearing the familiar call on all sides and only obtain one or two shots.

On October 19th I had my first attack of fever, which was not severe and soon yielded to phenacetin. It was however, rather a disappointment for I had taken five grains of quinine regularly every day since arriving in the Congo. The fever ran the same course that it used to do in India ten years ago but as it only once appeared in England during that period, I hoped it had gone for ever. Hundreds of mosquitoes hummed around with the ambitious idea presumably of carrying the germs to some other unfortunate.

As we shall now leave the French frontier and travel altogether in State territory we send the Senegalese escort down the river back to their station at Mobaie. The sergeant who was in charge was a most responsible man and was evidently held in great respect by the Chiefs of the French villages through which we passed. One day a

---

(1) Now in the British Museum (Natural History).

The River near Banzyville.

Chief was greatly disturbed because two men from his village had migrated into State territory. Although this is against the law it is apparently not a very unusual occurrence. Generally these emigrants have committed some crime and are fleeing from justice. One Chief, however, at Banzyville stated he had left the State territory because he objected to working rubber and had returned because he objected still more to paying the tax in the French Congo. It is impossible indeed to say which side gains by this emigration but it is very evident that it is not altogether one-sided and not great enough to affect seriously the size of the population of either the French or Free State Congo.

In Yakoma the people are paid chiefly by beads and salt and it is interesting to watch the long string of workers filing to the office of the Chef du Poste on Saturday, each one carrying a plate, a tin can or some other receptacle in which to receive his wages.

On October 22nd we decide to pack up and move on. The skins of the larger birds the toucans, razor-bills and serpent birds are keeping very badly but those of the monkeys, leopards and antelopes are in better condition. It is however, doubtful if they will last, for to preserve them it is necessary to hang them out in the sun every day which is obviously impossible when travelling. As a small native war is in progress higher up the Uele, Mr. Van Luttens kindly arranges to accompany us for the first three days in order to ensure that relays of paddlers shall be forthcoming for many of those gentlemen have forsaken the wooden blade for the iron lance. We are therefore a large party on October 23rd when we leave Yakoma

in a drizzling rain, the remains of the usual nightly tornado.
Although the paddlers wear no clothes and do not hesitate
to jump into the water at any moment it is curious that
they dislike rain very much and never work so well as
when a hot sun is shining.   The least diminution of temperature indeed affects them very much and they sit drow-
sily over the fire hugging themselves, being aroused to
action only with difficulty.   We number now about two
hundred including the thirty soldiers and armed capitas,
but as the current is not very strong we make good
headway through somewhat flat and uninteresting country
until we arrive at Prekissa, a large village on the north
bank of the Uele.

Here we were received by the Chief of the Abira tribe,
a great potentate who sat in a long hammock chair
surrounded by courtiers and ministers squatting on the
ground and holding spears of state on each side of him.
Having welcomed us he escorted us through the village
which is of great extent and well arranged.   Opposite his
square hut or palace is the Guard House in which are a
few soldiers armed with cap-guns for he has some independent authority and the power of life and death in
certain limited cases.   Behind the palace are many rows
of round huts close together.   Not a soul is visible or a
sound heard for these are the quarters of the wives of the
Chief and except the official lady who acts as legal queen
none are presented to the white men.   The present Chief
is a keen commercial man and understands the advantage
of being on good terms with the State for he has a large
rubber plantation and also works metals.   The blast
furnace is most interesting.   It is simply a pit about two

feet wide and deep formed by banking up clay and earth for several feet around which has been dried by the great heat of the furnace into a hard stony substance. Indeed at first sight the pit looks like a hole dug in solid rock. In it is placed iron stone and wood charcoal which is lighted and a blast made by several pairs of bellows formed of antelope skins. The molten metal is not run off but remains with the slag in the pit until it is cool when the latter is chipped away and the shapeless mass of iron is ready to be worked into spears and lances by the blacksmiths. Probably this method is a very ancient one indeed, and it is curious that it should resemble so closely the modern Bessemer process for making steel. Having walked through the village we return to our camp on the river bank and the Chief presents spears. He then proceeds to ask for anything he takes a fancy to in return. We had already given him cloth much more valuable than his lances when he suddenly demanded tobacco. I gave him the contents of my pouch and he then asked for that also. He next asked me to give him my jacket and finally wished to buy my cap for two ivory finger rings. To receive a present from a Congo chief is thus a very expensive honour. He then sat down and smoked while we eat, for it is contrary to custom to ask a native to dine at the same table as a white man.

We start again next morning at 6 a. m. The banks of the river are now assuming an equatorial appearance for we are in the third degree of latitude and palms grow in great profusion but the country is flat and uninteresting. About midday we land at Gembele, a large village with an extensive plantation. The Chief is a young, good-looking man with refined European features and a very gentlemanly manner. He owns a large island, many iron and copper mines and is very wealthy. When one was introduced to him he pointed with pride to the State medal he was wearing round his neck, a medal which is given to all Chiefs of whose election or succession the Government approves. An important feature of this village is a round enclosure built of trunks of trees and roofed with leaves which serves as a Chamber of State wherein discussions take place and justice is administered. Gembele only succeeded his father a year ago and among other responsibilities he has. to take care of numerous wives, step-mothers and aunts, the legacies of his father and uncles. They seem, however, to be well-disciplined for they were sunning themselves when we suddenly appeared round a corner but at a wave of the hand of the boy of the Chief, they all rushed for cover and not one turned round to try and catch a glimpse of the white men. Possibly they have peep-holes in the walls of their huts for it would be too much to expect them to have no feminine curiosity. Gembele is evidently respected by his people but he has a somewhat serious look as though he felt the cares of his position heavily. There is a strong rapid opposite the village so we allow the canoes to go up empty and enter them again above it. It is now intensely hot and progress is slow but we reach the village of Sembile before sundown and pitch our tents in a clearing. The huts here are still round and the people practically nude but the custom of wearing beads has disappeared and very few are painted.

There is a bright moon which acts here as a clock by night as the sun does by day. As the latter passes practically straight overhead it is astonishingly easy to tell the time within half an hour after a very little practice. It is more difficult to use the moon as the point of the hour-hand and requires some care. This, however, is the only means the sentry has of determining 5 a. m. when we wish to be roused for he could not read a watch.

We start again at daylight and ascend the river to Voro where we land with all baggage for the rapids here are so strong that it is necessary to walk for several miles. We therefore start in a procession of more than one hundred people along a narrow foot-path while the crews take up the empty canoes. The guide leads and I follow next, hoping to shoot any game that may exist in the neighbourhood before it is disturbed by the bearers. It is, however, speedily apparent that with the exception of birds it will not be possible to see any game at all for the grass is very thick and about eight feet high. After a time my gun weighs heavy so I give it to a bearer and a moment after two fine pheasants rise a few yards away. All around is evidence of game. Great tracts through the grass where the stately elephant has passed to drink at the river, spoor of buffalo and antelope at every water course and yet not a sign of life now for the sun is high up and a hundred bearers are yelling and singing close behind. After walking for about two hours we reach forest and enter its welcome shade. A small stream prattles cheerfully along under the trees and as the path several times passes through it we keep our feet comfortably cool. About 2 p. m. we reach a village beautifully situated on a slope in the midst of dense forest. This is protected on all sides by a strong stockade twelve feet high for leopards abound and when game is difficult to find do not hesitate to enter villages and carry off people. Here we halt for lunch and then on again through the forest full of cuckoo pheasants. These are not much more difficult to shoot than hand reared birds at home although they fly higher to clear the tall trees. They do not, however, appear to travel very quickly but this may be a delusion as it is difficult to judge distance in Africa. No other game birds come within range. Late in the afternoon we reach Bogosi, a large clean and well arranged village. The Chief is a pleasant fellow perfectly willing to sell us food for our party and monkeys, tortoises or anything else we may desire for ourselves. Here we change all our paddlers the present ones going back to their villages. As the tribe is at war with one higher up the river, Mr. Van Luttens thought it might be difficult to obtain paddlers here and so came himself. With his aid, however, the difficulty vanished for he arranged with the Chief that the paddlers who took us to Djabir should not be called upon to do any more work for the State for nine months. That is to say that the enforced forty hours a month would work out at six or seven days paddling in nine months and as each man was liberally paid in cloth no one could possibly say that he was used hardly. Having bathed in the swiftly running river we dined in the enclosure which did duty as the Council Chamber and then thoroughly tired turned in early.

It was not until 9 a. m. in the morning that we could make a start for all the baggage had to be fitted into the canoes and the paddlers arranged in their places. The first day with new crews is always a trouble but this is never repeated for the native has a good memory and every

bale, bag, gun and even small articles like books are taken
from the canoes each evening and put back in identically
the same place in the morning. This is remarkable
when one thinks that some hundreds of separate articles
have to be placed in one of seven or eight different canoes
in one particular place.

The river is heavily in flood for this is the end of the wet
season and the current is very strong indeed. Soon we
come to the first rapid and one of the men drops his pole
overboard at the critical moment. The other two, however, hold the canoe up by pressing against the rocks
while the water whirls past within an inch of the edge of
the little craft. At a word from the capita one of the
paddlers jumps into the rushing water, rescues the pole
and lands safely with it on the bank, fifty or sixty yards
below. All the Sangos swim like salmon but cannot of
course leap up rapids. They however, swim so powerfully
that they steer clear of the rocks and reach the side even
in the swiftest current. On we go slowly struggling up
rapid after rapid and when it is impossible to paddle and
pole the canoes against the stream the crew stand on the
rocks and lift them up. Sometimes the drop is three feet
at one spot and it is perfectly marvellous how these men
can thus stand waist deep in the water. Naturally we
ship a good deal of water which wets everything through
and through but the crew take this as a matter of course and
bale it out at intervals while the boys take care the firearms
are not injured. The amount of actual work the crew do
must be enormous yet they never seem fatigued and sing
as lustily at the end as at the beginning of the day. At
length we pass the island of Mutemu and seek for a place

for a camp.   There is not much choice for the forest is very dense here and it is necessary in every place to clear the undergrowth before the tents can be pitched.   Then fires are lighted and all are soon asleep.

We start again at daybreak and at once commence the fight with the rapids. Soon after a Chief appears in a canoe, and having explained that he is at war with a neighbouring tribe hopes it will not inconvenience the white man. On being asked why he is fighting he states that he has lost two women and thinks they have been stolen.   I then told him war was a mistake and I hoped he would make peace as soon as possible, at which he looked a little surprised and answered that he expected to be successful and capture several women as well as men.

The navigation of the Uele at this part of its course is so difficult that there are very few villages on its banks for the native who lives near a stream hardly ever walks and he will not settle unless he can travel by canoe.   For this reason there is often no pathway at all between villages only a mile or two apart on the river bank.   The few people there are have probably never seen a white man for as far as one can ascertain no one has been up here for ten years. However, where there is a village the Chief comes on board and presents a chicken.   About midday the kitchen canoe paddles by with fire alight and pot boiling. Soon after Chikaia shouts : *Le cuisinier est tombé dans l'eau,* and a little way ahead is seen a canoe apparently upside down close to the bank and twelve or fifteen black heads bobbing up and down in the water.   Mountmorres is just ahead in his canoe and easily within reach but to my surprise his paddlers suddenly turn away from the bank and make for mid-stream evidently straining every muscle. Turning round I order my crew to pull rapidly to the rescue but to my disgust they also turn into mid-stream and take no notice of my command. Having asked Chikaia the meaning of this he replied : *La petite bête qui mange l'homme.* Chikaia's knowledge of zoology and French being somewhat limited every animal is for him either a « *petite* » or a « *grande bête* ». The information was therefore not very valuable for it was impossible to imagine what small beast was in the habit of eating people. Thinking, however, of a crocodile I took my rifle but Chikaia laughed and said : « *Non, non, la petite.* » By this time we were well out in mid-stream opposite the kitchen canoe which—to add to the mystery—was not upset at all. The cook, the crew, the goats and the fowls were all, however, in the water. No danger was apparent for the crew were swimming at their ease and hoisting the live stock back into the canoe. It is useless being astonished at anything in Africa and there was obviously nothing to do but sit still while the crew raced along as fast as they could paddle. In a few minutes they pulled into the bank and there we waited for the kitchen which presently appeared with the cook reclining in the arms of one of the crew and moaning : « *Je mort, je mort.* » After a rapid examination, however, I could find nothing at all the matter. At length we discover the truth. His canoe had run into a large hornet's nest hanging from the branch of a tree and he had been stung in the head. To avoid further damage, he and the whole of the crew not only jumped into the water themselves but threw all the live stock overboard as well, for the natives believe that the sting of this insect kills and they fear it

more than an encounter with a wild beast.   The cook
was therefore in a highly hysterical condition and no doubt
in considerable pain also although no mark of a sting
could be discovered, amidst his thick curly black hair.
Still I took him into my canoe, gave him whisky internally
and bathed his head with permanganate of potassium and
he was quite well next day.   After this delay we struggle
on until just before dark we reached the worst rapid on the
river the Kandoko Falls, up which the canoes are lifted
inch by inch.   Everything was already wet so the fact
that a terrific to nado burst before we could pitch the tents
added but little to our discomfort.

On again at daybreak and after one or two ineffectual
attempts to negotiate the last strong rapid on this piece of
the river we conquer it and reach smooth water.   In the
course of the morning a canoe intercepts us in which is a
native dressed as a State capita and armed with a gun.
He says he has been sent by a white man to tell us not to
sound our tom-toms as it will attract the hostile tribe and
they will attack our camp.   We ask for the letter for white
men never send verbal messages by natives and when it
was not forthcoming became suspicious that our visitor was
spying our strength.   We told him that we were peaceful
travellers, that we should beat our tom-toms as much as
we liked and camp where we wished and that if the tribe
attacked us we should defend ourselves.   Probably our
rifles made an impression for we were not molested at all
during the day and at night camped in the village of the
hostile tribe.   Our paddlers indeed fraternised with the
enemy, against whom they would have been fighting if
they had not been employed by us.

THE SULTAN OF DJABIR.

The usual tornado burst in the night and we did not
make a start until 7 a. m. when we continued up the river
and passed several villages before 2 p. m. when Djabir
came in sight.   The view of the town from the distance is
very pretty indeed.   In the centre is an old fort with four
towers now partly demolished and on each side the houses
of the officials stretching along the river bank.   Here we
land two hours afterwards and feel that at last we shall
have a night's rest without fear that our habitation will
be blown away or soaked with water.

CHAPTER VIII.

Across Uele.—Djabir to Ibembo.

Djabir is a disappointing place. Although very imposing from a distance it is being rebuilt at present and at
close quarters it becomes obvious that some of the old
houses are in a very bad state of repair. Some welcome
newspapers meet us here and Im a delighted to learn that
the Government has passed the Licensing Bill and that the
Japanese are still successful. The Sultan of Djabir sent
his brother a young gentleman who has been educated and
speaks French, to present a small ivory war-horn and to
demand several times its value in cloth. Afterwards he
sold us some other articles but, although he received full
value for them he repented of his bargain next day and
demanded them back again. Of course we let him take
them. The Sultan himself seems to be equally difficult to
deal with and although the State has given him the rank of
Captain in the Force Publique and tried to humour him in
every way he is not a good subject. His village has the
usual characteristics with some signs of Arab civilisation.

Lord Mountmorres is now anxious to hasten to Bumba for the rest of the mail and if necessary to send a special courier to Coquilhatville with a cablegram while I arrange to follow more slowly and hunt the country in between. He therefore leaves Djabir on October 31st taking only one boy and a little baggage. It is a very hot day and at night-time a heavy tornado bursts over the Post. I wake up in a pool of water for the roof leaks badly and by bad luck just over my bed. Having moved this to a dry spot it is possible to sleep but not for long for the mosquito net was fixed to the wall where I left it forgetting the little pests. It is now a question of bites or water and as the latter seems cooler I replace the bed and fixing the roof of the net on the slope so that the heaviest part of the shower will run off, pass the rest of the night in comparative comfort. It is indeed time the place was rebuilt for at present Djabir has a depressing air of former greatness and present decay. As there are no elephants near and the antelopes are very small, I arrange to leave on November 1st but on starting to repack find many of the antelope skins are rotten and order them to be thrown away while the native lances and spears are covered with red rust and have to be cleaned, smeared with palm oil and repacked.

I start next morning to cross Uele, but as it is impossible to obtain more than thirty five porters some of the baggage has to be left behind. The loads are carried here in rather a curious manner. The porters make a band of coarse grass fibres and pass it over the crown of the head which is inclined forwards. The band is attached to the bale or box which itself rests on the back between the shoulders. Then leaning forward the porter, carrying

50 lbs, walks at $3\frac{1}{2}$ miles an hour over rough roads for
three or four hours with scarcely a stop.   Having crossed
the river the caravan is formed and at once strikes along the
path through the villages on the opposite bank to Djabir.

We are now on a frequented route and the villages and
people show far more signs of the influence of the white
man than those on the Ubangi.   The huts are square,
thatched with leaves and have verandahs while most of the
men and many women wear clothes.   The tatouage also
is here very different for the vertical line on the forehead is
not seen and a horizontal line of small elevations just
above the level of the eyes is very common; there are
however, various other devices on the cheeks and the lobes
of the ears are sometimes pierced for the insertion of a ring
of ivory nearly as large as a serviette ring.   The natives
are very polite, every single one giving a salute so that at
the end of a long village one's arm aches with returning it.
Chicken and eggs can be bought here for cloth at about the
price one pays in an expensive shop in London.   Some of
the natives said nothing and were satisfied while others
grumbled but did not take back their goods.   One man sold
nine eggs for about 2/-of which only three were fit to eat
and demanded 4/-for a chicken little larger than a pigeon.

The natives here seem to have been spoilt by the whites
who must have given them very high prices for food at first,
and these have never been reduced.   Naturally demand
and supply affect the price considerably.   A native refused
to sell us a duck at Coquilhatville for 14/-, for ducks are
rare.   On the other hand in remote villages rarely visited
by white men, the people will sometimes give two chickens
for an empty wine bottle and would practically sell them-

selves for salt so fond are they of that substance. This
they eat alone and relish immensely for the native salt is
very unpleasant. It is made from water lilies and certain
forms of grass which are burnt slowly under a fire, the
resulting ash containing a large quantity of sodium chloride. It is however, mixed with sulphur, charcoal and
other impurities and to remove these the ash is placed in
water when the sodium chloride and other soluble salts
enter into solution. This is then evaporated to dryness
in the sun and forms native salt.

Once clear of the line of villages which extend for two
or three miles, the path enters dense forest and the walk
becomes pleasant. Palms are abundant and the « parasol »
tree very common. Overhead are pigeons, a few ducks
and, as usual, thousands of parrots. I shot a few either
for the larder or for their skins all of which fell in the
dense undergrowth. Without a retriever these were no
doubt difficult to find but it was curious that the birds
with beautiful feathers and indifferent flesh were always
picked up while the ducks and pigeons usually could not
be found. All the porters returned along this path the
next day and perhaps were then more successful and
enjoyed the game which would not be harmed by hanging
for a day in a tree. The road is a good one being sometimes five or six feet wide and most of the marshes and
streams are crossed by rude wooden bridges formed by
trunks of trees laid parallel to each other.

Most of the way is up a gentle incline for we are now
passing over the ridge which separates the watersheds of
the Ubangi and the Congo. At intervals along the road
are small clearings in some of which are capitas armed

WARRIORS AT DJABIR.

with cap-guns to protect the rubber caravans from thieves. About midday we reach Kaki - kaki, a clearing in the forest in which is a mud house for the use of white men passing through and here I call a halt for we have marched about twelve or thirteen miles.

On again next morning at daybreak the path continuing through the forest, and as it is quite cold at this hour and the exercise is pleasant we march briskly only stopping to shoot occasionally.   After leaving Kaki-kaki the streams flow south instead of north which shows that after fighting our way up rivers for four months we have now reached the highest point of our journey and are at length going down hill.

It is indeed a great relief to think that instead of struggling up rapids, when next we take to canoes we shall be whirled rapidly down stream.   There is, however, nothing like a mountain or even a considerable hill in this part of Uele.   After an hour or two the forest ends and we cross a plain covered with grass only four to six feet high on which clumps of trees and bushes are dotted about.   On every side are traces of elephant, antelope and wild cattle but the sun is now high on his brilliant course and only man is foolish enough to work in the day time in Central Africa. It is indeed very hot marching for there is no shade and it is necessary to change the gun for the umbrella.   In another hour we reach the string of villages constituting the territory of the Sultan of Enguetra who like the Sultan of Djabir is not a particularly good chief. His people, however, receive the porters kindly and give them bananas.   Then on again under a very fierce sun until the north bank of the Likati river is reached.   Here we

enter a canoe and are rapidly paddled down the stream
which is only about twenty yards wide, until we reach a
clearing in the forest in which the Post of Enguetra is
being built by Lieutenant Gaspard.   In a few weeks
he has constructed a fine brick house of two storeys with
a large verandah looking down a natural avenue to the
river.

At this time of the year—the early days of November—
the Post is practically an island for the river flows on one
side and on the other three water is standing in the forest
to the depth of three or four feet.   This is no doubt good
for the rubber vines but bad for hunting.   However, I
determine to settle here for a week or two and hunt the
forest and plains about.   Next morning herefore I start at
5 a. m. in the dark and follow the guide who evidently
feels the cold and steps out at a good pace.   After passing
through the plantation we strike into dense forest and the
walking becomes very difficult.   Roots of trees below,
branches and vines above have to be dodged all the time
and it is a relief to march along the bed of a stream even
if it has two or three feet of water in it.   It is impossible
to see for more than a yard or two on each side through
the dense undergrowth and the sun and sky are quite
invisible although patches of lights show that the former is
now well above the level of the tallest tree.   Traces of
elephant and antelope abound, the former being of small
size without points worth having.   After two hours we
reach the plain and find the water nearly six feet deep.
There is no place about to pitch a tent and it is extremely
difficult marching in the forest in the night, but the only
chance of an elephant is to be here an hour or two before

daybreak. Indeed it is almost impossible to hunt until the water subsides and that means waiting for over a month. However there are plenty of small beasts and birds so the day was not altogether wasted.

The Congo is undoubtedly the land of exaggerations Everything here is bigger or smaller than any where else. If the elephants are the largest in the world the insects are the smallest and Enguetra is especially favoured by their attendance. Millions of little beasts fall on one all day long. Soup might here be called hexapoda bouillon and a glass of wine in a few minutes becomes a tincture of insects. Butterflies are especially numerous and are of great beauty. They are so lazy or sleepy that one can nearly always pick them up with one's fingers. Ducks are not agile creatures on land but here they waddle slowly up to the butterflies and as often as not catch them in their beaks.

The native is a curious mixture of simplicity and cunning He is very fond of strong alcohol but does not care much for wine. The mess boy here apparently stole some whisky and instead of filling the bottle up with water added red wine to the requisite amount. Of course the colour led to instant detection and of course he knew nothing about it, but he lurched about violently as he waited at dinner and it was obvious the new European drink was acting rather forcibly. It is very troublesome to have to lock up every bottle when travelling, yet it is absolutely necessary. There is, however, I hear a patent lock which can be fixed over the cork and is easily fastened to the bottle. This is worth remembering.

One day Chikaia stated that the Sultan of Enguetra intended to attack the Post that night and if he had done so it might have fared badly with us for we were only two white men with perhaps fifteen or twenty soldiers. However, a heavy tornado broke and perhaps the warriors refused to face the storm for nothing happened. The boys were very alarmed and did not hesitate to say so. As the relationship between the Sultan and the State was not very satisfactory the report might have been true, otherwise it might well have been idle gossip. War had then not been declared but the State soon after sent a force to occupy the district.

Chikaia, who is a Christian, formed a violent attachment to a woman who worked in the plantation here and asked to be allowed to marry her, although at the time she appeared to be the wife of a soldier with whom she was living. Chikaia, however, said she was not legally married, so we investigated the case. The supposed husband swore they were married, the woman swore they were not. The man, however, in this case evidently lied for he said the ceremony took place at a certain Post and was conducted by a certain official. Now only Commissaires of Districts and Missionaries can legalise marriages and the official named was neither. After representing to Chikaia that the woman did not seem a very desirable wife, I gave my permission to his marriage, provided that the Catholic Missionaries, to which church he belonged, were willing to perform the ceremony for the woman was not a Christian. The woman was very pleased and thanked me in the native fashion by at once asking for a necklace of beads for a wedding present. The demand for « tips » becomes sometimes quite humorous. A native girl fell down and cut herself and one of the officials dressed the wound until it healed. The parents then came and asked for a tip and when the astonished individual required to know the reason said that the girl had been every day to have her wound attended to and she ought to be paid for it.

One day as I was sitting after lunch half asleep, a green and white serpent glided through the open door into my room. It happened that my guns were leaning against the opposite wall and I did not fancy jumping over the beast, so simply shouted. It then withdrew on to the verandah and I followed as quickly as possible with a gun. In the meantime Chikaia came running up and gave it several blows on the back with a heavy piece of wood. The sentry then appeared and before I could stop him cut off its head. The skin was thus spoilt which was a great pity as it measured more than ten feet in length.

As it was not easy to procure paddlers at Enguetra I decided to send on one of the boys Mavunga with some of the heavy baggage on November 17th and to follow him the next day. He was very nervous at the idea of travelling alone and wished to borrow a revolver, but this of course I refused. It is curious that these coast boys fear the natives of the interior so much and still more curious that the presence of a single white man at once restores confidence. It is indeed becoming more apparent every day that the natives have a very genuine respect and admiration for the Europeans and credit them with powers which neither they nor any other people possess.

I leave Enguetra on the 18th in a most comfortable canoe with an awning so high that it is possible to stand upright, a great luxury in canoe travelling. The Likati flows swiftly through dense forests and we glide down the rapids very quickly and comfortably. No villages exist along the banks and nothing is visible except the forest until we reach Kati-kati a clearing in which a mud hut has been erected for the convenience of travellers. I went for a stroll in the forest but after half an hour was stopped by an unpleasant palpitation of the heart. Although the distressing symptom passed away quickly it was obvious it might occur again and then I realised for the first time that I was very anaemic and that hard exertion would be impossible for some time. This was the more annoying for the country around was particularly rich in game. We leave at sunrise which is, however, concealed by a thick water mist and speed along until we reach Dzamba or Ekwanga-tana close to the point where the Likati and Rubi rivers join to form the Itimbiri. Dzamba is a transit port where cargoes are transhipped from canoes into a small steamer the *Milz* which plies between it and Buta the capital of Uele. As the *Milz* departed the next day I decided to travel in her and thus altered my original plan of descending direct to the Congo. The Rubi is about three times as wide as the Likati and also flows through dense forest which is only broken here and there by Wood Posts. Although the water is high and the current strong the *Milz* which is a twin-screw steamer, travels well and early on the third day we arrive at Buta. The Post is being moved and some brick houses have already been built, one of which is placed at my disposal. After settling in it I call upon Baron de Rennette, the Commissaire of Uele which is a very important District for through it runs the path to the Nile and it has frontiers both to French and

English territories.   The Lado Enclave, however, is
governed separately by a special official.

One now realises fully the extreme difficulty and expense
of transport across Africa.   Take for example a bale of
cloth shipped at Brussels and addressed to Bomokandi.   It
is very possible that this will be transhipped at Banana
into a lighter which will be towed to Matadi; secondly it
will travel by train to Leopoldville; thirdly by steamer to
Bumba beyond which point the larger vessels do not run;
fourthly by small steamer to Ibembo; fifthly by canoe to
Dzamba during which journey it has to be carried by hand
past some rapids; sixthly by the *Milz* to Buta and
seventhly by hand to Bomokandi.   Every basket of rubber
and point of ivory exported and every box of food or bale
of cloth imported is indeed constantly being transhipped
and then conveyed by various methods a few hundred miles
on its journey.   The example given is by no means an
extreme one, and many others could be traced in almost
any direction.   The reason is simple.   Although the
whole of Central Africa is traversed by rivers which even-
tually flow into the Congo, both the main river and its
tributaries are in places impossible to navigate owing to the
rapids.   Great efforts are, however, being made to overcome these obstructions.   Wherever possible railways are
being constructed and roads made to avoid them the
latest great work initiated being the automobile road
through Uele.   It is indeed impossible now to carry by
hand the great amount of merchandise passing up and
down the country, even if the natives were willing to
undertake the task.   This is, however, the very work they
dislike most and during my visit an immense quantity of

stores was lying at Buta and could not be forwarded
owing to lack of porters. The automobile road will
change all this, for trains of waggons carrying the merchandise will then be quickly and easily towed by road
engines. Passengers will also be conveyed in a similar
manner and it is reasonable to prophesy that in five or ten
years time it will be possible to cross Africa from the Nile
to Banana without travelling a single mile in canoes or on
foot.

At present the difficulty of transport chiefly affects the
comfort of the officials for their stores of food may be
delayed for some weeks and although it is possible to live
on kwanga, goats and chickens, it is not a suitable diet
for Europeans. Less difficulty is experienced with the
exportation, for the rubber and ivory are always travelling
down the hill towards the mouth of the river. Baron de
Rennette fully realises how extremely important it is to
have good food in this exhausting climate and took his
native cook to Europe to receive some lessons in the culi-
nary art. He has been rewarded for his trouble and now
lives almost as well as he could at home. Good food,
indeed, is almost as necessary in Africa as pure water.
After a hard day's work in this climate it is impossible
either to relish or to digest goat's flesh or tough chicken
and the result is weakness followed by fever, anaemia or
dysentry. When travelling it is still more difficult to
obtain properly cooked food, and it was thus especially
pleasant to find oneselt dining off a clean white cloth with
clean silver, hot plates and food cooked and served in a
manner which would have been a credit to a London
club.

There is a good path to Bima and Bomokandi and I
was thinking of taking this ten day's walk when an
attack of fever caused me to change my plans again.
While still at Buta Mgr. Derikx arrived.   He was on a
tour of his diocese and expected to be travelling for a year.
I was very pleased to see him and was bound to confess
that all he had told me of the Congo on the voyage out was
strictly accurate.   Having recovered from the fever and on
the recommendation of Baron de Rennette, commenced a
course of arseniate of soda, I left Buta on November 28th
in the *Milz*.   The small steamer rapidly descended the
river for the water was now falling rapidly.   Many crocodiles had ascended this small river to lay their eggs and
were lying on sandbanks but we travelled so quickly that
it was impossible to shoot them.   Near Buta is one of the
villages constructed for and by old soldiers and, like the
rest of these institutions, this one is very well arranged
and kept forming a striking contrast to the ordinary native
village.   It is indeed extraordinary how the savage can
be changed into a civilised being by a few years of military
discipline.

I reach Dzamba again on the 29th and continue the
journey in canoe on the next day.   The current is
running swiftly down the Itimbiri and after an hour we
arrive at a rapid and march through the forest while the
canoe descends without passengers.   The river winds
here very much so that although the current is very strong
it is more than an hour before the canoe arrives at the
village, which we reached walking, in about twenty
minutes.   The journey up is very slow and tedious
for the baggage has to be carried by hand along this

short cut through the forest. It is therefore proposed to build a light railway to relieve the native of this task.

I reach Ibembo on the 30th and am met by Lieutenant François, the Chef du Poste. It is a large station with a big mess for many travellers are continually passing through. On this date three hundred and fifty soldiers with their officers were marching through with the object of occupying Enguetra and its district until the Sultan becomes a little more reasonable. It is very difficult for the troops to avoid ambuscades in the forest. They march in a hollow square formation with the women, who carry much of the baggage, in the centre. Each soldier carries a knife and literally cuts his way through the undergrowth. If the head, flanks or rear of the square is attacked the men close up and meet the enemy with a steady fire for they always march with the rifle loaded. Progress is naturally very slow and the enemy difficult to catch, while the chance of being hit by a poisoned arrow or a lance hurled from behind a tree is always present. The soldier however, is very plucky and well earns his twenty-one cents each day, and the one franc twenty-five cents a month which is reserved for him.

Next day I visit the Catholic Mission of Ibembo and am received by Father Benin who is in charge in the absence of Mgr. Derikx. The Mission is situated on a plateau about 200 feet high on the opposite bank to the Post, but a little lower down the stream and the whole place is admirably arranged, the view across the river being especially beautiful. Three hundred natives, mostly children, are engaged in the plantations and gardens all being dressed in a pretty uniform and appearing healthy and

The Itimbiri River.

happy. There is indeed, very little sickness here, for the buildings and grounds are as scrupulously clean as those of a State Post. In a well-fitted carpenter's shop the entire furniture for the chapel and houses has been made from the wood of old canoes which is hard and well-seasoned. The boys also work in ivory, turning serviette rings with great accuracy and skill. Four or five brethren and five sisters form the staff of the Mission and one of the latter superintends the cooking with most happy results.

Next day I walk through the native villages near Ibembo where most of the men fish and the women make pots of clay. There are a great number of children about and very little sickness. Sunday as usual was market day and the people from the neighbourhood brought in kwanga, fish, eggs, chicken and three antelopes. Food is sold for mitakos three of which will purchase enough kwanga to feed a man and woman for a day. In the afternoon a Chief arrives with the not unusual story that a troup of elephants have entered and destroyed his plantation of manioc. We arrange therefore to start at 4 a. m. next morning on the chance that they will repeat their visit, but a heavy tornado in the night renders hunting impossible. After spending a pleasant week at Ibembo, I prepare to descend the river to Bumba and then to ascend the Congo to Stanley Falls.

BASOKO FROM THE RIVER.

CHAPTER IX.

Ibembo to Stanley Falls.

The *Delivrance* a steamer built on the same lines as the *Florida* arrives at Ibembo on December 5th with a large cargo of cloth, clothes, beads, salt and other articles for barter, and also cases of food for the Europeans. This is almost her last voyage up the Itimbiri this season, for soon the waters will have fallen so low that the river will be navigable only by canoes. No time is wasted in the Congo State. As soon as the cargo was discharged, the empty holds were filled with baskets of rubber and ivory and in less than twenty four hours after her arrival, the steamer was ready to depart.

Having arranged to travel by this boat, my baggage was soon on board, and we left Ibembo at midday on the 6th of December. At first the river passes between the cliff fronting the plateau, on which the Mission stands and low lying forest on the opposite bank. The cliff is red, and is evidently full of iron. In a short time however, both banks become flat and are covered with forest broken at intervals by villages which are well arranged, clean and tidy. Some of them are wood posts, and one is occupied by old soldiers, who have built themselves very good houses. These veterans have no pension, but are given materials to form plantations, and also supply the steamers with wood at the usual rate. They rarely, if ever, return to their native villages, which they left seven or ten years before as naked savages, for they are now smart civilised men and imitate the appearance and manners of the Europeans as closely as possible.

About 6 p. m. we reach the Post of Mandungu, situated on the right bank of the Itimbiri. It is very well built and scrupulously tidy. Behind is a high wooden stockade, and in front, along the river bank is a small wall broken by a kind of arbour, in which is a brass gun with the interesting inscription G. R. III 1799.

On again at daybreak down the swiftly running stream. The Itimbiri indeed, like its principal feeders, the Likati and Rubi, is rapidly falling, for the dry season has now commenced in earnest, and although thunder-storms are frequent, they are not accompanied by rain. We stop at Moenge, a small post on the left bank of the river, for the mail, and then on again until the Congo is reached an hour before sunset. The great river is still very full of water, which shows no signs at present of falling. This is, only to be expected, for all the tributaries are now emptying themselves into the main stream, which is thus kept high for some weeks after they have commenced to fall. We turn down the Congo and after passing some villages and a post of the S. A. B. Trading Company, reach Bumba at sunset.

This is an important shipping port, for the large vessels stop here owing to the difficulty of navigating the Congo higher up. All the cargo for Stanley Falls and the Upper Congo, as well as that for Uele, has therefore to be transhipped here. The place is designed in a series of squares, one side of each being formed by the river while the spaces thus left are filled with well kept gardens, the whole being very effective. Mr. Simon, the commandant of the Station kindly lends me a house and also arranges to allow the *Delivrance* to take me up to Stanley Falls as soon as her cargo has been discharged. On each side of the Post are villages extending along the river bank. The men here wear a loin cloth, but the women only bangles, and the tatouage is varied and extensive.

Next day the *Delivrance* was charged with sheets of corrugated iron for building purposes and it was very interesting to watch the natives carrying these to the ship. Like some civilised people, the natives are so lazy that they often give themselves a great deal of work in the effort to avoid it. The plates were of various sizes and shapes and consequently of various weights. Sauntering slowly up to the stack on the beach, one of the porters would examine it carefully and search for as small a load as possible. Then he would either lift the upper ten or twelve plates or try to pull the one he had chosen out from the stack.   Having accomplished his object thus with great exertion, he would put the plate on his head and carry it leisurely the few yards to the boat.   Of course the larger ones had to be moved some time, and in reality at the end of the day the lazy fellows had thus done more work than was necessary.   Compared with Hindu or Chinese coolies, the Central Africans indeed both in the plantations and at the dock side, accomplish rather less than half the amount of work in the same time.   The paddlers, on the other hand, cannot be called lazy, and when propelling canoes against strong currents or up rapids, exert themselves to the utmost.

We leave Bumba on December 9th in the *Delivrance* and turn up stream.   After passing the mouth of the Itimbiri the banks are unoccupied for many miles, dense unbroken forest lining each shore.   Here and there is a wood post and we pass also two considerable areas which had evidently been cleared some time ago and occupied by villages.   The people, however, were very troublesome in these parts and have since migrated into the interior leaving the ancient sites to elephants and other beasts. It is very much more comfortable on the *Delivrance* than on the larger steamers, for, being the only passenger, I have plenty of room in the cabin below and as usual in these small craft, we have all our meals on the bridge.

On the 11th we arrive at Barumbu, a small Post with a large brick house for the Commissaire when he visits the place.   Here most of the natives were dancing and looked very ridiculous.   They did not move over the ground and seemed to be doing a kind of physical drill.   First one leg

LOADING A BARGE.

was kicked forwards and backwards while the other did a heavy stiff looking hop. Then perhaps the arms were thrown up and down and the whole body advanced from the hips, and finally the head was jerked to and fro. These movements were repeated time after time, evidently in a regular set order, for once started, several people performed exactly the same in perfect time whether they could see each other or were back to back. The whole affair looked stiff and ungracious, but was keenly enjoyed by the natives.

GENERAL VIEW OF BASOKO.

An hour later we arrived at Basoko, the capital of the Aruwimi District. It is different from other Posts, for it has a wall running along the river front with a square tower in the centre, giving the appearance of fortification. There are indeed a few guns here, but not many troops. After paying a short visit to the Commissaire General of Aruwimi, Captain Pimpurnieaux, we continue our journey.

Next morning was pay day, all the ordinary seamen receiving 21 mitakos a week, but the capitas and wheel-men were given more. These latter are usually a very responsible set of men, for after a few journeys they remember every island and land-mark on the river and often steer all day without a word of command from the captain. About midday we met the *Ville de Paris* which differs from the other steamers in having her wheels at the side instead of at the stern. This arrangement has not however, proved a success, for this boat is neither so fast nor so easily steered as the others.

I am now troubled with a new complaint, synovitis of the knee joint with a good deal of effusion, which makes it very difficult to walk. It is curious why this malady should have appeared, for I had not knocked or otherwise injured the joint and had indeed been sitting quietly on steamers all day for the previous week.

On the afternoon of the 12th we reach Isangi, a Post at the junction of the Lomami and the Congo. This river drains the territory occupied by the Company of the same name and we turn up it to visit Ilambi, the chief town. There are a few large villages on the banks where the natives exhibit a curious method of hair dressing. It is allowed to grow long, which is very unusual in the Congo, and is then turned up and matted together on the top of the head with grease and the red powder of the cam-wood. The effect is, that each appears to be wearing a red and black cloth cap.

We reach Ilambi, which is a large Station well built and very tidy, the next day. The Company leases a very extensive territory along the river banks and does a large trade in rubber and ivory, the Brazilian variety of the former growing here very well. The natives are quite satisfied, work well and give very little trouble, although it is necessary to punish them sometimes, and as usual, the prisoners on the chain are given work to do outside the prison. We stay here one day and then descend the Lomani, and turn up the Congo. The banks of the river now have a new appearance, for they are higher and no longer densely wooded and at short intervals are villages thickly populated and containing a high percentage of children. Most of the men fish or build canoes, and all the people seem to be constantly trading with each other, selling food or curiosities for mitakos or cloth.

We stop for the night at Yonanghe, a Post which has been built by a true native of the Congo, who at one time was the boy of Inspecteur d'Etat, Malfeyt. He has travelled to Europe, speaks French and English and makes an excellent Chef du Poste, which rank he enjoys officially, with all its rights and privileges. Everyone agrees he is thoroughly responsible and a very good friend, but if a captain of a steamer offends him, he will not sell him a chicken or even an egg for any sum.

On the 15th we reach Yakussu, where is a Mission Station of the English Baptists. As I cannot go ashore. the missionary, Mr. Stapleton, comes on board and we have an interesting chat. He has known the Bangala District for many years and has seen the riverside population diminish very much during the last fifteen years. This he ascribes partly to the Sleeping Sickness and partly to emigration to the State Posts. At first it was very difficult for the people to raise enough food for themselves and for the soldiers in the Posts, and to avoid the hard work, many accepted service under the State. Here however, near Stanley Falls, there is plenty of food and the people have no difficulty in providing for their own wants and in supplying the State Posts as well. He thinks that after the cruelty of the Arabs, the rule of the white man appears as heaven to the native. All are therefore contented and happy, and as there is very little Sleeping Sickness, the population is increasing. The Mission boys are taught to be carpenters, masons and brick makers, for food is so plentiful that there is no need to establish plantations. The chief grievance of Mr. Stapleton is, that the Government will not permit the missionaries to settle where they wish and will not grant them land. Several other missionaries have also complained of this, but some districts are certainly not civilised at present, and it would be dangerous for any white man to live in them without a military guard. It thus happens that while there are a great number of Mission Stations along the Congo in the part where the population has diminished greatly, there is not a single Mission on the State side of the Ubangi river where the people are very numerous.

We arrived at Stanleyville in the afternoon. The town is situated on the north bank of the river and consists of streets of large well built houses with much space in between which is laid out in gardens. On the opposite bank are the works of the railway to Ponthierville, a number of corrugated iron buildings and a large native village. In front, a hundred yards up the river, the lowest of the Stanley Falls can be seen, the white foam glistening in the sunlight as the water rushes over the rocks.   The Commissaire of the District—the Province Orientale—Lieutenant De Neullemeister, kindly lends me a house and acts as my host.   Fish is very plentiful here, but a sudden and terrible disease has suddenly carried off most of the goats and chickens and we are therefore, rather short of fresh meat for a few days.

Many of the natives have the Arab type of features and their village is quite Arabian in appearance.   They are all very civilised and work well, so that much rubber is collected, although the population about Lake Tanganika is not very dense.   The women here are clothed and do not work in the plantations at all.

Next day Lieutenant De Neullemeister and I, cross the river and are met by Mr. Adams, the Director of the Railway Company.   We enter a truck and proceed along the new line which plunges into dense forest immediately, turning and twisting in many directions in order to avoid the numerous soft places and ravines and although there are a few steep gradients, most of the way the line runs on fairly level ground.   The soil is a kind of ferruginous clay in some places and sandy in others and all the bridges are constructed of wood.   Mr. Adams says the natives are good workers and that they have had no trouble with them and very little sickness.   The guage of the line is considerably wider than that of the Matadi-Leopoldville railway and at present about thirty kilometres have been finished the whole passing through thick forest with clearings here and there for the huts of the workmen. The difficulties of construction are very great, but these are being surmounted and the cost of transport of material is enormous, for every steel rail six of which weigh a ton has to be carried from Europe to Matadi by ship, then by the railway to Leopoldville, and then up the river for nearly a thousand miles. The Company has its own private steamer, the *Kintamo*, a stern wheeler of 500 tons which is the largest vessel on the Congo, but like the rest was carried out in sections and put together and launched at Leopoldville. The construction of this railway will thus be costly, and it is doubtful if the amount of produce carried will be sufficient for some years to pay a dividend. The advantages of it will however, be very great, for at present the falls render the river useless for navigation, and everything has to be carried round by hand. Everywhere indeed, there is evidence that the State not only spends enormous sums in opening up the country, but welcomes the formation of private companies who will help them in their gigantic undertaking. It is difficult to realise that probably no man, white or black, has ever set foot in the forest a few hundred yards away, and yet we are travelling smoothly along a steel railroad through a tractless desert of trees propelled by a modern steam locomotive. The line does not pass near a single native village, for this part is not thickly populated and the only creatures whose paths are interrupted, are the elephants, buffaloes and wild pigs. On our return we visit the house of Mr. Adams, a solid structure of brick and European cement, and the Mess of the thirty or forty whites employed on the line who live here very well for mutton as well as goat can be purchased from the natives. The price of everything which has to be carried from Europe is very high at Stanleyville for the cost of transport is very

great.   In the afternoon, we make a tour of the town, and
as it is impossible to walk, I am conveyed in a kind of
bathchair resting on one wheel.   One boy goes in front and
one behind and when the road is very bad or an obstacle
is met, they lift the machine bodily over it.   It is however,
a bumpy ride, for the roads are very rough and the chair
has no springs.   We pass the Mess, capable of dining
sixty men and visit the prison.   This is a brick building
arranged as a quadrangle with an exercising yard in the
centre.   The cells are lofty and airy and only one prisoner occupies each, but many sleep in one dormitory.
Everywhere great cleanliness is observed, so that one is
not altogether surprised to learn that the mortality due to
Sleeping Sickness is very small among the prisoners.
Some of them are making mats and baskets in the yard,
but most are working on the chain outside.   In a separate
building, the women, who also wear light chains, are
cooking dinner for the prison.   Indeed, on the whole the
lot of a prisoner in the Congo is better than he would be
likely to experience in a native village, with the exception
that he is compelled to work.   Most of the people are sentenced for theft or violence, but one woman was imprison-
ed for throwing a solution of pepper into the face of her
husband and nearly blinding him.   There is a separate
room set apart for white prisoners, but it has not yet been
used and is at present much more satisfactorily occupied by
the instruments of the band of the Force Publique.

Near the Mess we pass the house of Tippo-Tip, a small
mud structure with a verandah and a roof of grass.   It is
not used at all now, but is allowed to remain as an histo-
rical monument.   Stanley was compelled to negotiate with

Tippo in order to avoid a conflict at the time when the State was not sufficiently armed to undertake such a task but since then, Arab rule has been entirely driven from Central Africa. Almost opposite the Falls, a fort is being constructed with a ditch all round. When finished, it will be capable of holding the whole garrison and supplies for eighteen months. It is of course, only constructed as a defence against native attacks and is not built strong enough to resist big gun fire.

The quarters of the Force Publique here are very comfortable. Each man has a room to himself about seven feet square constructed of brick and the sergeants have a small house, each containing two rooms and a verandah. I looked into one or two and they were well arranged. Bed and mosquito curtain, table and chair with a few pictures and ornaments, showed what an advance the native had made in civilisation since he slept in a hut on the mud floor.

Finally we visited the motive power which enables all this to be done, the rubber stores. Here people were busy sorting and packing the precious material into baskets ready to be carried to the Barge which was waiting to sail.

CHAPTER X.

Stanley Falls to London.

The prison gang arrives at 8 a. m. on the morning of December 18th and at once my baggage is carried down to the river and placed on board the Barge. It is a novel sight. A long line of prisoners chained together, slowly marching down the road with bales, boxes, chairs, tables and portmanteaus on their heads. No method could be simpler or more secure for transporting baggage. The Barge—as the name implies—has no means of propulsion and depends for her locomotive power upon a powerful steam tug which is attached alongside. The whole space in the ship is thus devoted to cargo and only passengers who are sick are carried, the accommodation being limited, but there is a fine deck on which to sit or walk about. The Barge is of about 400 tons burden and is therefore as large as the mail passenger boats, and the great advantage of travelling in it is, that since there is absolutely no vibration or motion to be felt, it is very comfortable for writing.

As the navigation of the river is difficult near Stanley-ville, a pilot takes all the boats down the first day's journey and returns in the next vessel ascending. On the way we called at the Catholic Mission for one of the priests who wished to travel to La Romee and I was astonished to find he was quite ignorant of the agitation against the Congo, which was taking place in Europe, and wondered, as many of us do, what was the cause of it, for he knew nothing of atrocities or cruelties to natives.

Afterwards we stopped at Yakussu for wood and then at La Romee where there is an extensive farm. Here we take on board some fresh vegetables and cow's milk which however, is not fit to drink an hour afterwards. The climate in the Congo is very bad for all kinds of food. Antelope, killed in the early morning, is often rotten by the evening, and thus the difficulty of obtaining fresh food is greatly increased. The rapidity with which flesh decomposes is, perhaps, the reason why the natives prefer it in that condition, for as it is so difficult to obtain meat fresh, they may have acquired the taste for it rotten, just as some civilised people train their palates to prefer game high. It is however, very disgusting to see them eating. One day a carcase of a wild pig in a highly decomposed condition was picked up by one of the paddlers on the Ubangi. This was cut up and shared among the canoes and part of it fell to my crew. Next day a most unpleasant smell accompanied us all the forenoon and no one could detect the cause, in fact, none of the natives noticed it. At lunch time however, the polemen produced a basket full of rotten flesh which they had stored in the

THE FORCE PUBLIQUE AT STANLEYVILLE.

front part of the canoe and thus given me the full benefit of it. As they commenced eating it raw, it was rather too much and I promptly ordered them to the other end of the boat where I could neither see nor smell them.

After travelling rapidly all day down stream, we tie up at sunset at Yonanghe and ship some rubber. We start again at daybreak, but as the wood in this part is both plentiful and good, the captain stops frequently at the posts and takes a large amount on board. This is a wise precaution, for lower down the wood is not so good and there is less of it, while there are more steamers to be supplied. At most of the villages the natives come to the beach with goods for sale, but the price of curios is too great here to tempt me.

On the 20th we reach Basoko after running through a terrific tornado with so much rain that for a time it was impossible to see the banks. It is supposed to be the dry season here, so this storm is presumably an exception. Every morning there is a fog on the river more or less dense, which lasts for an hour or two after sunrise. During this period, it is often necessary to steam dead slow, for it is impossible to see a boat's length ahead.

A pathetic incident happened one day. We were transporting eight prisoners to Boma and when we stopped these carried wood on to the steamer. One of them was the son of the Chief of a large village at which we stopped, who thus had the mortification of seeing his heir working « on the chain. »   He begged the captain to liberate him, who of course had not the power to do so even if he had wished, for the man had been sentenced for a serious theft and was now on his way to a convict settlement.

The Chief therefore, told his son he was to give no trouble to the authorities and tried to comfort him by saying he would see the railway and Boma and the great ships which went to Europe.   These prisoners gave no trouble at all.   They were fed on the same food as the crew and did a certain amount of work, the only sign that they were criminals, being the chain which bound them together.

On the 21st we reached Bumba and shipped a good deal of coffee.   Here it was necessary to give the *chi-cotte* to one of the crew for continually shirking work. He was given twenty five lashes, but it did not seem to affect him physically or morally, for immediately after-wards he smiled, rubbed himself and then slowly walked ashore to carry bags of coffee and while his fellows were hastening to finish their task, he was deliberately loitering about.   Next time he will be dismissed and then he will find it difficult to find employment.

On the following day we stopped at Dobo, one of the Posts of the Mongala Company, which has been taken over by the State.   The Company found it was very difficult to make the people work and some serious charges of cruelty were proved against the officials.   The Bangala tribe are however, very savage and only a short time ago a trader was killed and his body cut up ready for eating when some troops arrived and rescued it.   The Government therefore, sent a punitive expedition into the country.

There are very few villages on the river, and no signs that there have ever been any, for the forest grows to the water's edge in an uninterrupted line.   At sunset we arrived at Lisala, which is a large military training camp, well constructed and managed.   In it about a thousand

savages are being converted into clean, smart-looking
soldiers.

Next day we passed the « Kintamo », which was forcing
its way up against the stream with a cargo of rails directed
to Stanleyville.   On the 24th we stopped at Mobeka, which
is situated at the point where the Mongala river runs into
the Congo and was the chief post of the Mongala Company.   It is surrounded by a brick wall, except towards
the river, and access to the Post from the native village is
through stout wooden gates.   At one place is a kind of
watch tower built on the wall and the whole gives the
appearance that the occupants knew they were living in
the midst of cannibals, who would not hesitate to attack
them if they were not well prepared to resist.   It is to be
hoped that the present expedition will be successful in con-
verting a few from their barbarous condition, but great
difficulties have to be overcome, for the fighting must be
in the forest, as the natives never meet troops in the open
if they can help it.   In the evening we reached Nouvelle
Anvers, a large and populous town.   The houses are
arranged along the river bank, surrounded by gardens,
and the quarters of the troops leave nothing to be desired.

Christmas Day has nothing resembling Christmas about
it.   A tropical sun burns overhead, warm sandy water
glares below.   In the morning we pass Mosembe, a Mission Station, and in the afternoon, Lulongo.   There used
to be a large village and coffee plantation here, but it was
not a success and has been abandoned.   The Mission
however, still remains as also a Wood Post where we stop
for the night and try to believe that duck is turkey and
mutton, roastbeef.   We have now traversed the whole of

the river which runs past the Bangala District. It is undoubtedly very sparsely populated, but on the other hand, there are no remains of villages or clearings in the forest which would indicate it has ever been otherwise.

Next day we reach Coquilhatville early and after taking some rubber and gum copal on board leave in the afternoon. From this point the river is familiar and at each place are old friends. At Irebu, Commandant Jeniaux comes on board and we have a chat about the condition of the agitation in Europe. Since we last met I have travelled some thousands of miles and have formed an opinion both of the system of Government and of those who administer it. There is no doubt whatever in my mind, that the native is not habitually ill-treated and that he is very well paid for his work. It is impossible to do more than guess at the object of the outcry, but it is certain that no agitation based on such a little foundation has ever been attended by such a near approach to success.

Next day we stop at Lukolela and take on board logs of wood and timber already worked into beams and posts for building. A little lower down is the old coffee plantation and close to it, tobacco is being grown. The river here is very wide and full of islands. To one of these we tie up and are at once attacked by millions of mosquitoes, who will not allow us to eat our dinner in peace. Fortunately I find an old pair of kid gloves and with my head covered with a silk handkerchief and my legs in high hunting boots, prepare for the onslaught. The mosquito here bites through duck trousers and socks with great ease, but his trunk cannot reach through the thickness of a sleeve of a coat and a flannel shirt, so with suitable clothes, one can

gain a little peace, except for the constant humming round
one's ears.   A cigar or pipe is no protection at all, but
the insects will not face the smoke of a wood fire.   Since
people cannot either, however, that is not much use.   As
it was, the few bites swelled up badly and completely upset
the theory held by many, that after a few months in the
Congo, the mosquito bite has no effect.   It is some grati-
fication—but not much—to think they only gained an
extract of goat and chicken, instead of a solution of good
juicy fresh meat.

On the 29th we passed Yumbi and Bolobo.   At the
latter place great numbers of natives came to the beach to
trade with our crew and black passengers who bought
dried fish and kwanga.   In the evening we reach Sandy
Beach, opposite which, is « Lonely » Island so called
because it is the last island on the river before it narrows
to pass through what is known as the canal.   Here the
banks are flanked with hills which are a welcome sight
after the dead level of the forest higher up.

Next day we arrive at Kwamouth and after taking some
cargo from the Kasai on board move on to a large Wood Post.
It is not a very interesting or lively occupation watching
people cut wood in the forest and stack it on the beach,
and these Posts are sometimes used as places of punishment for refractory Europeans, whom it is thought desirable to isolate for a time.   The strict paternal system is
carried out throughout the State and methods of punishment are adopted which are rarely if ever found elsewhere.
For minor offences the Europeans are fined by stopping
their pay for a certain number of days and sometimes
a man is revocated, which means he is sent home without

being paid for the six months or year previously. In this way men who drink hard when they have the opportunity, who are habitually insubordinate, or who are undesirable, are weeded out rapidly. Penal offences are of course tried in the Courts and punished with imprisonment. It is indeed curious after travelling in America and our colonies, to find, sturdy, rough, independent characters behaving with extraordinary meekness and docility. Drunken brawls and promiscuous revolver shooting are unknown in the Congo, for the simple reason, that it is impossible up country to procure drink. There are no drink shanties or gambling dens and indeed no amusements of any kind. Men work from 6 a. m. to 6 p. m., have their dinner and go to bed. Very little news penetrates from the outside world and conversation is therefore, limited to the immediate affairs of the individuals concerned. Small matters thus appear to be far more important than they really are and the story of any little adventure soon becomes magnified out of all recognition. This, perhaps, accounts also for some of the absurd stories of atrocities.

On the last day of the year we reach Leopoldville and are comfortably installed in the Inspector's house. A kind of fête is held in the evening and a procession passes with lanterns on poles, but there is very little singing or noise of any kind and the whole affair is rather ghostly.

On January 2nd we leave Leopoldville by train and remembering the amount of the fare coming up, I was careful to reduce my baggage to the minimum. Of course the food cases were all empty, the wine drunk, the salt paid away to natives and the petroleum burnt; still for myself, three boys and excess baggage, the fare for the

two hundred miles was over £25. Just before we left
Leopoldville, who should enter the carriage but Mr. Joseph
Clarke, of Ikoko, and another Mr. Clark, who is also
a Missionary. I was very pleased to see them and hear
the news from their side of the question. They were
travelling to Matadi to attend a meeting of missionaries,
but to-day only proceeded as far as Kinshassa.
Mr. Clarke told me he had sent to the Commission of
Enquiry some new photographs of the boy without a hand
whom he had shown to me at Ikoko and was convinced
that the world would be startled when the report appeared.
All the meetings of the Commission are held in public and
therefore the evidence submitted at them is already known.
The interpretation of this apparently depends upon the
already formed opinion of the individual, for while the
State officials say that very little, if anything, has been
proved against the Government, the Missionaries are quite
satisfied that the A.B.I.R. Company will be severely con-
demned. Of course no report can possibly satisfy any
of the controversialists for their feelings are too strong to
permit them to be content with cold facts judicially stated.

After an uneventful and uncomfortable journey through
the beautiful part described before, we arrive at Sono
Gongo about 5 p. m. and take a room in the Magazins-
Generaux, a wooden building raised above the level of the
ground and fairly clean. It is beautifully fresh and cool
up here, and for the first time for half a year, it is possible
to take a bath in clear white water.

On again at 6.30 a. m. at which hour it was quite cold,
but as the sun rose and we descended, it became very hot
indeed, for we were then well south of the Equator and it

was summer in the Lower Congo. The scenery through the Palabala mountains improved, if possible, on a second acquaintance and the railway as a feat of engineering, appeared still more marvellous. After a dusty, hot journey, we arrived at Matadi at 5 p. m. and found Mr. de Rache, the Commissaire of the District, on the platform. He had kindly taken a room at one of the hotels, but as it necessitated climbing up the hill and I could only walk with difficulty, I decided to sleep on board the *Anversville* which was discharging cargo at the pier head. Here indeed were all the luxuries of Europe. A barber, a big bath, white spotless table-cloths, clean shining plate, red juicy beef and last, but by no means least, cold drinks. It is worth roughing it to experience the keen delight at returning to comforts which are never appreciated at their full worth when enjoyed every day.

Next morning we leave Matadi for Boma in the *Heron*. The current is running down through the narrow channel at about ten knots an hour and the water roars and bubbles as though passing over rocks in a rapid. We therefore roll a good deal and travel very fast indeed until we reach Boma just before midday.

Stories in the Congo grow with extraordinary rapidity and my attack of synovitis had been converted into a serious illness before it reached the capital. A room had therefore, been prepared at the *Croix Rouge* in which I was soon comfortably installed. The hospital consists of eight sets of rooms arranged in four buildings, separated from each other, but with the verandahs connected by balconies. In the centre is a building in which the eight sisters live the whole thus forming a † with a building at each end of the lines and one where they intersect. The whole is situated on a hill from which a magnificent view can be obtained of the river and country around. Here I remained for nearly a week and was attended with much skill and care by the medical men and sisters. It was necessary to make some calls in the town and a carriage at Boma was placed at my disposal similar to the one at Stanleyville, but travelling in it was more comfortable for the roads are better in the capital. It was very hot and the mosquitoes were terribly hostile, but otherwise my visit was very pleasant and agreeable.

On January 6th the German cruiser the *Vineta* and the gunboat the *Habicht* entered the Congo and the Governor General gave a dinner to the officers to which I received the honour of an invitation. I am tempted to give the menu to show that although living in the Upper Congo is not good, as a rule, in Boma it is possible to give a banquet worthy of anyone.

MENU

—

Potage aux tomates

—

Coquilles de crevettes

—

Barbue. Sauce câpres
Pommes nature

—

Filet de bœuf
Flageolets. Pommes rissolées

—

Asperges de Malines
Sauce au beurre

—

Pigeonneaux rôtis. Petits pois

—

Poulets farcis. Compote de mangues

—

Canetons rôtis Salade russe

—

Gâteaux
Ananas au kirsch
Fruits. — Desserts

The wines were Oporto, Hochheimer, Niersteiner, Pichon Longueville 1893, Château Grand Larose 1893, Corton and Louis Roederer Champagne. The dinner was served admirably by native boys while the band of the Force Publique performed in the garden.

The strong, grasping instinct of the native was well shown after I had paid off the « boys, » written them good characters and made them handsome presents. At the last moment they all came and demanded a further tip which I rather indignantly refused to give. However, they showed by their manner then that they were well satisfied and knew very well that it would be very difficult to obtain such high wages again. I had many long talks with Mr. Vandamme, who was as usual, very hard at work, and Mr. Underwood who kindly helped me to settle many matters. Indeed, everyone with whom I came into contact, whether State Officials, Missionaries or Traders, were always extremely kind and courteous and converted what might have been a very unpleasant and dangerous journey into a most interesting tour and I sincerely hope that all will remain, as I hope they are now, good friends, whether they agree with me or not about the merits of the system of Government in the Congo.

After bidding farewell to the residents at Boma, I left in the *Wall* on January 10th and after a rapid journey to Banana, joined the *Anversville* which immediately put to sea and by sunset the mouth of the Congo was out of sight.

The voyage home was uneventful, except for a few days of strong head winds. Among the passengers were Mr. Gohr, the Director of Justice, who well deserved a holiday after his extremely responsible and arduous duties, Captain Stevens, the Commissaire of the Equator District, as cheerful and jolly as ever, Mr. Longtain, the Director of the A. B I. R. Company who has come in for a quite unmerited share of abuse, and many other State Officials, many of whom were in an indifferent state of health. Two or three Catholic and some Baptist Missionaries were also travelling home and it was interesting and satisfactory to find that everyone, whether State Official, Missionary or Trader, was convinced that the Commission of Enquiry would issue a report which would correspond with his own opinion.

There was plenty of time to arrange the impressions of the tour in order and to formulate some general ideas on the system of Government in the Congo and the manner in which it is administered. The whole system has been created and is controlled absolutely by one mind. It is a very simple and extremely practical machine, but it is very vast. The officials who work it therefore, have each their own special task allotted to them and very few appear to understand the principles on which the whole moves. The problem which has been faced and successfully overcome, is how an unknown land populated by savages can be developed and civilised by its own resources without heavily taxing the native and without poisoning him with alcohol.

It is done in this manner. Each native is compelled to do a certain amount of work for the State. This results in the collection of great quantities of rubber and ivory for which the native is paid. The rubber and ivory are then sold at a profit in Europe and the sum so realised is used to pay the heavy expenses of transport, to keep up the Government and to open out new lines of communication throughout the country. The native is thus made to work instead of paying a tax in money and it is possible to raise enough revenue without selling him alcohol.

As has been shown in these pages, the native is very grasping and very idle and has little idea at present of the value either of produce or work. He thus charges an extortionate amount for his goats and chickens, and demands heavy fees for services rendered. The State however, fixes the price of labour and food at its fair value and demands a certain amount of one or other from each village. This sometimes leads to discontent and rebellion just as do the taxes levied by other Governments, and it is necessary to occupy territory with troops. No soldier however, is allowed to have in his possession a rifle unless he is accompanied by a white officer, and if he tries to ill-treat the natives, is severely punished.

The officials themselves, are subjected to the most severe

discipline, and as they exist, so to speak, on the rungs of a ladder, each one can be punished by the one next above him, who is, in turn, responsible, until at length the summit is reached. Every Post is worked on identical principles and the responsibility for its success or failure, rests with the official in charge. He is not permitted to try experiments or to alter the system in the least degree, and can only use his moral power to influence the natives. The question has been asked whether this system is not contrary to the letter or spirit of the Treaty of 1885. Clause V. of that treaty runs as follows. « No Power which exercises or may exercise sovereign rights in the above mentioned regions shall be allowed to grant therein either monopoly or privilege of any kind in commercial matters ; foreigners without distinction shall enjoy protection of their persons and goods as well as the right of acquiring and transferring moveable and immoveable property and the same treatment and rights as subjects of the nation in the exercise of their professions. »

In the first place it must be remembered that the Berlin Act applies to all the Powers possessing territory in the Congo basin and not to the Free State particularly, and secondly, that it was agreed upon by the Powers to prohibit monopolies and privileges in commercial matters and to suppress slavery, but not to interfere with the Government of the States or Colonies which were then or might be established and which might or might not sign the treaty. All the Powers indeed which signed the Act of Berlin of 1885 did so voluntarily and among them the Congo Free State which had already been recognised by the whole of Europe as an independent State. The signatory Powers to that Act did not create, define the boundaries, or in any way particularly specify the Congo Free State which is bound by it, therefore, to the same extent only as is England, France, Germany, or other signatory Powers. All these Powers at various times have declared that vacant land is Crown property. A German Imperial Order of November 26th 1895 says that the proprietorship of all vacant land in German East Africa belongs to the Empire. An Order issued by the Commissioner of the French Congo of September 26th 1891 runs « Uncultivated soil and vacant land which nobody legally claims shall be considered as belonging to the State and shall form part of the colonial domain (1). » In the British Empire, the right of the Government to declare vacant lands in the colonies Crown property has been frequently exercised (2). In annexing all the vacant lands, the Congo Free State therefore, has only followed the usual custom practised by all countries, so that it is obvious these lands are absolutely the property of the State, which, therefore, has a perfect right either to sell or lease them to Companies, Missionaries or Traders, or to collect the produce from them itself.

Indeed it was never intended that the whole Congo Basin should be pegged out into claims by a host of adventurers without any system, law or order, for such a proceeding would have speedily led to complete anarchy. Since then the vacant lands belong to the State, it is obvious that traders can only acquire landed property either from the State,

---

(1) See *New Africa* by Senator E. Descamps, p. 73 *et seq.*
(2) In Canada, Australia and the North West.

from other traders or persons possessing land. Again it is obvious that a trader only has the right of purchasing the produce of the land from the owner and although he may buy for example, rubber, which a native Chief has grown on his own plantation, no Chief may go into the forest which is State territory, collect the rubber from it and sell it, for such would be simple robbery.

Now the State imposes regulations upon the concessionary Companies and traders, which it also observes carefully itself on its own land in order that the rubber plants shall not be killed and furthermore it stipulates that all who take rubber juice, shall plant young rubber trees and vines to replace those which die in process of time. The supply of rubber is thus assured in the future. In spite however of the most stringent rules the officials of the private companies undoubtedly ill-treat the natives sometimes.

What then would have been the result if the country had been parcelled out among a number of private traders, who had simply pegged out claims? Their object would have been to make a large fortune and return home as soon as possible. After a few years, therefore, all the existing rubber trees and vines would have been bled to death, no new ones would have been planted, and the native would certainly have been over-worked and ill-treated. The country would then have been deserted and left to return to savagery. The State itself on the other hand is working for the future. Everything which can grow is planted, the natives are daily becoming more civilised, Posts are being built, roads and waterways opened up and the whole place rendered beautiful and attractive.

In the meantime, property in the country is guarded,

trade is perfectly free, and everyone, native and foreigner, is free to pursue his business in his own manner, subject only to such laws as are imposed in all civilised countries for the good of the community at large.

The Congo Free State has indeed, without breaking any Treaty, solved the problem which has baffled the combined wisdom of all the ancient great colonial Powers. It exists on its own resources without poisoning the natives with alcohol; it extracts much wealth from the soil without fear of ever exhausting it; it opens up great tracts of land without running heavily into debt, and – noblest of all – it daily converts naked cannibal savages into self-respecting responsible people.